THE
MONTESSORI
HOME

Create a Space for Your Child to Thrive

THE
MONTESSORI
HOME

Create a Space for Your Child to Thrive

ASHLEY YEH, M.ED.

Publisher Mike Sanders
Senior Editor Ann Barton
Art Director William Thomas
Senior Designer Jessica Lee
Proofreaders Lisa Starnes, Monica Stone
Indexer Celia McCoy

First American Edition, 2022
Published in the United States by DK Publishing
6081 E. 82nd Street, Indianapolis, IN 46250

22 23 24 25 26 10 9 8 7 6 5 4 3
003-325757-JAN2022

Published in the United States by Dorling Kindersley Limited.

Library of Congress Catalog Number: 2021943594
ISBN: 978-0-7440-4569-7

DK books are available at special discounts when purchased
in bulk for sales promotions, premiums, fund-raising,
or educational use. For details, contact:
SpecialSales@dk.com

Printed and bound in China

Illustrations by Jill Labieniec
Photographs pages 83, 100–123, 134–139, 145 © Hapa Family, Inc.
All other images © Hannah Quintana

For the curious
www.dk.com

For my incredible husband and our amazing children,
who continue to inspire me to learn and grow.

CONTENTS

8   Introduction
10 About Maria Montessori

12 THE ESSENTIAL TRIAD
14 The Prepared Adult
18 The Prepared Environment
22 The Child

26 THE BEDROOM
28 Infants
32 Toddlers
36 Preschoolers

38 THE BATHROOM
40 Infants
42 Toddlers
46 Preschoolers

48 THE ENTRYWAY

52 THE KITCHEN
54 Infants
55 Toddlers
58 Recipes for Toddlers
60 Preschoolers
62 Recipes for Preschoolers

64 THE DINING AREA
66 Infants
70 Toddlers
74 Preschoolers

76 THE PLAY SPACE

78   Designing the Space

82   Selecting Toys & Activities

86   Choosing Books

88   Shelf Rotation & Toy Storage

90   How to Organize a Shelf

92   How to Arrange a Work Tray

94   How to Present an Activity

96   The Infant's Movement Area

98   The Montessori Mobiles for Infants

100   Infant Activities

107   Toddler Activities

116   Preschool Activities

124 THROUGHOUT THE HOME

126   Introducing Practical Life to Infants

128   Practical Life for Toddlers

136   Practical Life for Preschoolers

142 THE GREAT OUTDOORS

144   Infants

146   Toddlers

148   Preschoolers

150   Common Questions

154   Montessori Furniture & Materials

155   Recommended Reading & Resources

156   Index

160   Acknowledgments

160   About the Author

INTRODUCTION

The funny thing about this book is that it isn't really about your home at all. At its core, this book is about your child. It's about understanding how children use their environment to fulfill their own potential and understanding your distinct role as you guide them on their path. It's about cultivating a new perspective, one that engenders deep respect for your child as a human being and creates more joy and harmony in your life together. And as we explore each room of your home throughout the chapters that follow, you will begin to see the world quite differently. You'll see it through your child's eyes.

Just like so many of the stories that other parents and caregivers across the globe have shared with me, my own journey into Montessori came about by happy accident. As a new mother of a six-month-old baby, I found myself on one sunny afternoon during her nap time researching local daycares and preschools in preparation for my eventual return to work as a public school teacher. Discovering that there was a local Montessori school nearby, I suddenly recalled my own long-forgotten time as a child in a Montessori elementary program. As many fond memories began to resurface, I felt a subtle but determined shift in my focus as a parent. I *knew* in my heart that I wanted a Montessori education for my child.

Upon further research into the quality of local Montessori schools, I stumbled upon a few reviews from parents that talked about their experiences in applying Montessori principles at home. My curiosity was immediately piqued, and I tumbled headlong down an internet rabbit hole of how to implement Montessori practices from birth. This was the precise moment in time that my understanding and respect for children, and my perspective as a parent, was forever changed.

Over the last several years, the Montessori approach has not only become a lifestyle for my family, but it has also developed into a fervent passion in my professional life. I've been so fortunate to be able to share what I've learned along the way with thousands of other parents and caregivers all over the world. And every day, I am privy to countless inspiring tales of success, as families open their hearts and homes to the many benefits of the Montessori approach for their own children.

So why choose a Montessori lifestyle for our children? In doing so, we offer the freedom to move, explore, participate, and learn. We follow their interests as they grow and meet them exactly where they are, without trying to change them. And by setting up our homes to be accessible, with our children's independence in mind, we help them to feel confident, joyful, and respected. Given the freedom to be curious and creative, they naturally cultivate a love for learning. In the long term, this guides our children toward becoming happy, self-disciplined individuals who feel confident about who they are, have a sense of their role in society, and want to contribute to the greater good of the world.

Although the Montessori approach is most commonly associated with formal education, this book offers an accessible, practical guide for parents to set up their home in a way that fosters their young child's independence while supporting their needs, interests, and abilities. These ideas are applicable to homes and families of all shapes and sizes and are appropriate whether or not your child attends a traditional daycare or school, a brick-and-mortar Montessori school, or a home school. You can take heart in knowing that, at the end of the day, the greatest influence on your child's development will always be the rhythm and flow of life in your own home.

It was Dr. Maria Montessori who said, *"The child is both a hope and a promise for mankind."* And it is my greatest hope that this book will help to further spread the "Montessori love" across the globe, creating more joy for families everywhere and raising up the future of our own humanity, beginning with the way we parent our children at home.

ABOUT MARIA MONTESSORI

The Montessori method of education bears the namesake of its creator, Maria Montessori, who was a woman ahead of her time and a luminary of early childhood education.

Maria was born in the small town of Chiaravalle, Italy, on August 31, 1870. Her father was a financial manager with staunchly traditional values, while her mother was well educated and an avid reader, quite uncommon qualities among Italian women of the time. Much like her mother, Maria was a good student with a natural thirst for knowledge. As a teenager, she enrolled in an all-boys technical institute to prepare for a potential career in engineering. This was a decision made against her father's wishes, as his more conventional values dictated that Maria should have pursued a study of the classics, as did most other women.

In time, Maria changed her mind but decided to pursue medicine—yet another male-dominated field—instead, which was a most unusual aspiration for women. Although Maria did not initially gain entrance to medical school, she persevered by undertaking additional coursework to bolster her application and was eventually accepted into the University of Rome's medical program as the only woman in her cohort. When she graduated in 1896, she became one of Italy's first female physicians.

While her early career work was primarily focused on the fields of pediatrics and psychiatry, Maria's observations of intellectually and developmentally disabled children in the asylums of Rome led to her eventual interest in education and ultimately spurred her to question the established pedagogical practices of her time. In 1900, when she became codirector of a new training institute for special education teachers, Maria seized the opportunity to study her own ideas about education from a scientific perspective. She developed many of her own methods and materials, based on the work of Jean Marc Gaspard Itard and Édouard Séguin, for use with the children in the program. Many of the children made such remarkable learning gains that they were later able to pass public examinations commonly given to neurotypical children, and the program was declared a great success.

In 1907, Maria took on the challenge of opening the first Casa dei Bambini (Children's House), a full-day program intended to provide care and education for three- to seven-year-old children of the San Lorenzo district's poor working class. As these children were impoverished but otherwise developmentally normal, Maria was keenly interested in using the opportunity to test out her methods and materials and see if they would have a similar positive impact on the children's educational outcomes.

It was in this first Children's House that Maria observed behaviors in the young children that ultimately formed the foundation of her approach to education. She noticed that the children exhibited deep concentration, engaged in many repetitions of activity, and displayed a keen awareness and appreciation for order in the environment. She also discovered that the children possessed greater interest in practical-life activities or in the materials she had designed than in the traditional toys that were provided. The heavy furniture was replaced with lightweight, child-sized tables and chairs so that the children could move them of their own accord, and child-sized materials were made available for use on easily accessible, low shelving. Maria experimented with allowing the children the freedom to choose their own materials and activities and ensured that they experienced uninterrupted work and freedom of movement within the limits dictated by the environment.

It soon became apparent that the learning materials and classroom environment that Maria had prepared were helping the children to thrive. They transformed from unruly children into focused, independent, self-disciplined students with a zest for learning. Maria believed that independent work was an essential component of a child's sense of autonomy and self-motivation to learn. She also believed that children must be acknowledged as individuals and that by treating them in this way, they were better able to fulfill their own potential. The extraordinary success of the first Children's House attracted attention from distinguished educators, journalists, and public figures everywhere, and news of the "Montessori Method" spread like wildfire. Just two years later, the first Montessori teacher-training course was held in Italy, and by 1910, Montessori schools were opening up all over the world.

Over the next century, formal Montessori training programs were developed for infancy, as well as the elementary and secondary levels of education. Maria firmly believed that *"Education must begin at birth."* She wrote copiously about the crucial role of the parent at home in a young child's life. And so it has become widely recognized that the philosophies underlying the Montessori approach can also be successfully applied in the context of the home environment.

Maria spent much of her career writing, traveling, lecturing, offering courses, developing teacher-training programs, and expanding upon her approach. She lived through war and political turbulence and was even forced to remain in exile in India for several years, all contributing to her fierce advocacy for humanitarianism and social change. She spent her final years in Amsterdam, where she passed away on May 6, 1952.

THE ESSENTIAL TRIAD

In keeping with the old adage that "true beauty lies within," Dr. Montessori also unequivocally held that the real secret of childhood lies within the child. Thus, the successful implementation of Montessori practices at home will require a deeper understanding that goes beyond the superficial details of your child's play space.

Your journey must begin with looking inward to reassess your own perspectives about your child's development and capabilities—and this, on its own, is a paradigm shift for many. You must also learn to see your child's environment with fresh eyes, from their perspective, so that you are more effectively able to create simple, organized, and beautiful spaces that invite more meaningful learning and offer natural opportunities for independence. And finally, you must seek to understand and observe your child without judgment or interference, respecting them for exactly who they are in the present moment, just as

a scientist quietly observes the humble honeybee as it busies itself among the flowers.

It is quite possibly the most exhilarating challenge you may ever face as a parent, as you will come to see your child in a completely different manner. But your efforts will be greatly rewarded in the cultivation of a deep appreciation for your child's experiences as an individual, as well as a closer relationship based on mutual respect and unconditional love.

In this chapter, we explore the three basic elements comprising the foundation of the Montessori approach—the adult, the environment, and the child—and how they interact with one another so that you may gain a greater understanding of your unique role as a parent in preparing an environment at home that gently guides your child to reach their fullest potential.

THE PREPARED ADULT

You have the extraordinary privilege of being your child's first teacher in life. Every experience, every interaction, every aspect of your home environment . . . all are learning opportunities. You are your child's primary guide as they navigate what it means to be human.

But aside from fulfilling basic biological needs and offering your parental love and support, what else must be done? What does it mean to *prepare* oneself for undertaking the incredible responsibility of guiding your child as they construct themselves into their own individual? In her book *The Absorbent Mind*, Dr. Montessori says: "The real preparation for education is a study of one's self. The training of the teacher who is to help life is something far more than a learning of ideas. It includes the training of character, it is a preparation of the spirit."

This kind of preparation involves a direct confrontation with your own societally conditioned biases and prejudices against children so that you can overcome them in a concerted effort to offer your child the true dignity and respect they deserve. It also requires accepting the fact that your child is a highly capable being and recognizing the many ways in which you might be inadvertently creating obstacles for your child (for example, when we impatiently jump in to "help" our child without first being asked for help).

PRACTICE OBSERVATION

One critical step toward preparing yourself as a Montessori parent is to observe your child. Choose a time when your child is independently engaged in their own play or focused on some task of their choosing. Aim to quietly observe without interfering in any way so that your child's activity and direction are preserved, as if you weren't even in the room. Take note (either mentally or on paper, whatever feels most natural to you) of as many details as you can. Here are a few ideas for you: How is your child moving their body, hands, and fingers? What is their facial expression? Which kinds of activities are they gravitating toward? How long do they remain with each activity? Which kinds of activities are they not choosing? Are they completing an activity from beginning to end or stopping part of the way through? Are they experiencing frustration? How do they manage their frustration? How do they respond when they are successful? Which aspects of their selected work seem to be capturing their attention?

Keep in mind that the activity your child chooses may not be something you expect, like a toy. In reality, *activity* can be defined as anything that your child independently chooses to do, from running laps about the house to practicing pulling up on furniture, exploring the pots and pans in the kitchen cabinet, or examining stray crumbs on the living room floor. All of these activities are valid choices; what matters most is that your child has selected the work of their volition.

Taking the time to practice observing your child in this way will not only help improve your mindfulness as you learn to focus your attention on the present moment with your child but will also afford you a convenient "inside look" at your child's interests and abilities. By directly observing how your child chooses to spend their own time, you will become more knowledgeable of how to adapt the environment to better suit your child's needs. For example, if you observe that your toddler doesn't seem interested in the puzzles on the shelf and instead continually selects activities that involve building and stacking, then you may decide to remove the puzzles for a while and replace them with a variety of building materials.

SHOW RESPECT

Another step in your own preparation is learning how to offer genuine respect for your child in your everyday interactions. It is unfortunate that, in much of modern society, we are conditioned to disregard children based on the belief that they should obey adults without question because we know better and we're in charge. However, the Montessori approach offers a different perspective: our children are the future of humankind, and we must offer our support as they undertake the immense task of constructing their own intellect and personality.

One of the simplest ways that you can show greater respect for your child is to get down on your child's level when you're speaking with them so that you can make direct eye contact. You should also ask their permission before physically handling them in some way (even with babies): "May I pick you up now?" or "May I give you a hug?" And if your child ever requests that you stop doing something to them, you most certainly should respect their request by stopping.

Try to avoid interrupting your child while they are focused on a task; instead, wait until they've broken their own concentration (e.g., don't ask your child if they need to use the toilet while they're in the middle of playing with trains). And if there is a transition that needs to be made, it is respectful to offer a warning ahead of time: "We're going to leave the park in 5 minutes. Would you like to go on the swings or the slide one last time before we go?"

OFFER FREEDOM WITHIN LIMITS

Ideally, your child should be offered many of the same general courtesies that you might offer another adult. However, this does *not* mean that your child should be given free rein to do as they please. That would simply be neglectful, not respectful. Instead, the ideal approach is to offer your child freedom within limits. This means providing age-appropriate choices and opportunities for independence, while also maintaining clear expectations and setting limits whenever necessary.

This might look like allowing an infant to choose their own toy from a limited number of options in a basket or to choose which foods they'd like to eat from their plate at mealtimes. Examples for toddlers and older children might include choosing their own outfit (from two seasonally appropriate options), selecting toys and activities off the shelf (from a limited number that you've made available), and picking their own snack (from two healthy choices).

When your child inevitably tests the boundaries of the freedoms they have been offered, your role is to keep them safe by setting kind and firm limits. For example, if your child is climbing on the table, you might say: "I see you want to climb on the table. I can't let you climb up there because it's not safe. You can climb on these pillows instead." Give your child an opportunity to change their behavior on their own, and if they don't, then you can follow through by gently helping them (physically, if necessary).

PROVIDE FEEDBACK AND ENCOURAGEMENT

One final aspect of your own preparation to consider is how you provide feedback to your child about their accomplishments. Most adults in the current generation were raised on a steady diet of praise and rewards, either being offered a generic "Good job!" at every turn, earning a gold star on a sticker chart, or having adults respond with over-the-top exclamations about something that was actually quite ordinary: "Wow, I love your drawing, honey! You're such an incredible artist!"

The problem with this kind of praise is that it ultimately creates extrinsic motivation in

a child, instead of fostering their intrinsic motivation. The child begins to seek out praise from others in order to feel good about themselves and often abandons anything that feels too challenging, especially if the potential for praise or reward is removed. Over time, they effectively become *praise junkies*, whose primary motivation for any task is the reward itself.

In the Montessori approach, praise and rewards are eschewed in favor of encouragement and specific feedback. For example, instead of offering a value judgment, such as "What an amazing tower!", you can acknowledge their effort: "You worked really hard to balance your tower." If your child is excited about showing you their drawing, instead of responding with "It's beautiful!", you can offer specific feedback about what aspects of their drawing drew your attention: "I see that you used a lot of blue and yellow on this part." Or even turn the question around on your child: "What do *you* think of your drawing?" And if your child does something to help you, instead of saying "You did a great job, buddy!", you can simply offer a sincere sentiment: "Thank you, I really appreciate your help in keeping our playroom clean."

This doesn't mean that you can't *ever* praise your child or tell them that you're proud of them. There will certainly be times that this feels genuine and appropriate! The key is to make sure that authentic encouragement and feedback are your typical go-to responses so that your child's motivation, pride, and sense of accomplishment continue to remain intrinsic.

THE PREPARED ENVIRONMENT

The primary intent of a Montessori environment is to aid the child in their construction of both their personality and their intellect. A child uses the environment itself to accomplish this task; thus it stands to reason that the environment should be carefully prepared in an effort to maximize opportunities for independence and learning. As Dr. Montessori described it: "The first aim of the prepared environment is, as far as it is possible, to render the growing child independent of the adult."

The term *environment* is inclusive of all things a child might encounter during their explorations: not only the toys and activities on the shelves but also the various tools and materials that are available in other spaces around your home (e.g., child-sized kitchen utensils or gardening equipment), as well as the overall atmosphere of each space.

Dr. Montessori recognized that infants, toddlers, and preschoolers experience an intense *sensitive period* for order. We'll discuss more about sensitive periods in the next section, but for now, the bottom line is that young children thrive in spaces that offer organization and predictability. They have a developmental *need* to know that there is a place for everything and that everything will always be in its place. A space that is tidy, organized, simple, and real caters to this need. Everything in it exists for a reason, and the atmosphere conveys a sense of peace and tranquility. Conversely, if there are too many choices and a sense of clutter or chaos, a young child will easily become overstimulated.

This doesn't mean that your home must be immaculate at all times. Such an expectation is unrealistic, since real life is often messy. However, taking the time to do a bit of decluttering and purposeful organization throughout the various rooms of your home will allow your child to become more independent and feel at ease during their everyday explorations.

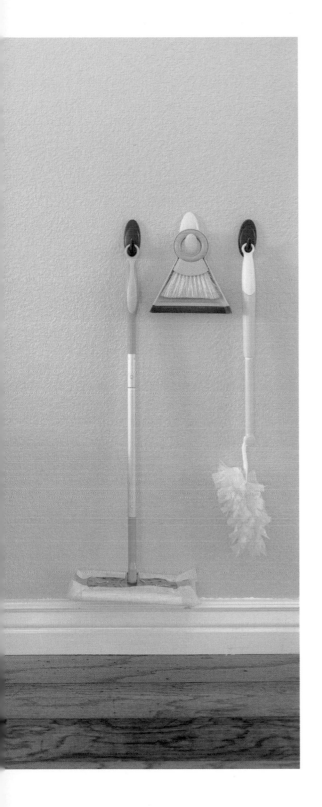

QUICK TIPS FOR DECLUTTERING AND ORGANIZING

- Start with the "easy" stuff: let go of any toys or activities that are broken (and can't be fixed) or missing pieces or which your child has developmentally outgrown.

- Consider donating any toys that are plastic, battery-operated, and do all the entertaining for your child. (For more detail about the reasons for this, see "The Play Space" chapter.)

- Sort the remaining toys into two piles: one that includes items your child is currently interested in or developmentally ready to use and one that includes items your child is less interested in at the moment (or items that are not yet developmentally appropriate but will be in the near future).

- From the "interested and/or appropriate" pile, choose a few items to place on your child's shelf. All of the remaining items can be temporarily stored away. (We'll discuss more about how to rotate your child's shelf in "The Play Space" chapter.)

- When decluttering the various rooms of your home, try to find "a place for everything." Focus on clearing away the visual clutter that tends to collect on surfaces (e.g., tables, counters, and shelves) by paring down visible items to only those that your family uses on a *daily* basis. Organize items that are only *occasionally* used into "hidden" storage that keeps it accessible but otherwise out of sight: organizer trays in drawers, boxes and bins inside cabinets or closets, extra storage inside of an ottoman, etc. And for any items that are only *rarely* used, store them in places like the attic, basement, garage, or the highest shelf in a closet. For anything that isn't used at all anymore, let go of as much as you can.

Having a limited amount of space at home can sometimes be construed as a disadvantage; however, the opposite is true—it actually works in your favor! The Montessori approach tends to overlap with many of the ideals of minimalism, most especially because a child's environment is ideally simple, uncluttered, and organized. A smaller space will encourage you to keep your child's collection of toys and activities to a minimum. Thus, with a little creativity and ingenuity, a Montessori setting can be created *anywhere*!

For example, you can use existing furniture and shelving in your home, such as the bottom shelf of a coffee table or bookcase, as your child's activity shelf. Or to keep things even simpler, you can create a "shelf-like" area by arranging your child's toys on the floor along a wall. You can still promote independence by having a single folding stool for your child to use whenever they need to reach the counter, but keep it folded and tucked away when it's not in use. Of course, these are just a couple of potential ideas, so remember to keep your eyes and mind open to the possibilities.

CREATE OPPORTUNITIES FOR INDEPENDENCE

Another essential part of the prepared environment is the intentional inclusion of opportunities for independence. Start by assessing your home room by room, looking for any small changes you can make that will help your child become more independent. A few questions to ask yourself might include: What activities does my child do in this room each day? Are the things my child needs neatly arranged and easily found, or do I need to do some decluttering and organizing? Can my child reach things by themselves, or are they placed too high? Can I rearrange anything using low hooks or shelves to help bring things down to their level? Would the addition of a step stool be helpful? Is everything in the room physically safe for my child to be independent, or do I need to add some safety features (e.g., install outlet plugs, secure heavy furniture to the wall, tie dangling up cords out of the way)?

Jot all of your ideas down on a piece of paper or in your favorite note-taking app. Tackle each of the items on your checklist gradually over time so as not to overwhelm yourself with trying to make too many changes at once.

BUILD A FOUNDATION OF REALITY

There is also a great emphasis on providing a foundation of reality in a young child's environment in order to help them assimilate their budding knowledge of the world. In Dr. Montessori's original children's houses, the environment was set up to include both real tools and materials *alongside* traditional items for pretend play, such as blocks, dollhouses, and pretend tools and cookware. But she discovered time and again that the children showed no interest in these pretend things, always seeming to prefer the real tools and materials that were available. Since these items were largely ignored, she ultimately removed them from her classrooms. This is the primary reason that, to this day, you will not find items for pretend play in traditional Montessori classrooms.

However, your home is not a classroom (unless you're homeschooling, and even then, there is still typically some separation between formal time for learning and your child's "down time"). In a properly prepared Montessori home environment, there most certainly *should* be various items and spaces available for imaginative, open-ended play, as this is a basic developmental need of all young children. There's more on how to set up these areas in the "The Play Space" chapter of this book.

It should be noted, though, that there is a difference between *reality-based imaginative play* (e.g., pretend cooking, doctor's visits, or caring for a baby doll) and *fantasy-based play*. Children under the age of six have a difficult time distinguishing reality from fantasy, which is why they are afraid of monsters in their closet and readily believe in the existence of unicorns. Ideally, you should try to steer clear of cartoons and pop culture references (e.g., Disney characters), anthropomorphized animals, and any other fantastical creatures until your child is developmentally ready to understand these concepts around six years old.

If elements of fantasy are introduced at an earlier age, then be sure to have ongoing conversations with your child about the fact that they aren't real. Otherwise, do your best to provide a solid foundation of reality in your home environment. As much as possible, choose toys and books that depict realistic representations of things that actually exist. And when it comes to Santa Claus, the Easter Bunny, and other fictitious characters, it is most respectful to be honest with your child. You can still offer to "play Santa" during the holidays if your child wishes to do so (this can be a good compromise if you're at all concerned that your child may feel "left out" of the cultural experiences of their peers), but be sure that you're not confusing your child by intentionally lying about their existence.

INCLUDE NATURAL ELEMENTS

Dr. Montessori also maintained a deep respect for nature. She observed that children are quite inspired by nature and possess an appreciation for beauty. Thus, natural materials are always preferred (over plastic) in a child's environment whenever possible, including materials like real wood, bamboo, glass, metal, ceramics, silk, and cotton. Incorporating elements of nature and beauty at home can also be accomplished by carefully selecting beautiful artwork for display at your child's eye level, offering fresh flowers on the table, and caring for houseplants.

THE CHILD

Out of the three elements that compose the foundation of the Montessori approach—the prepared adult, the prepared environment, and the child—it is the child who is arguably the most significant, for it is the child's own course of development that guides each of the other elements. The adult must first prepare themselves if they expect to be able to properly prepare the child's environment, as that environment must necessarily include developmentally appropriate activities. However, this can only be accomplished if the adult understands the child's developmental needs so that they can determine which materials to include. Thus, the most commonly offered refrain in the Montessori approach is to *follow the child*.

THE FOUR PLANES OF DEVELOPMENT

In Dr. Montessori's time, and even still today, it was a common assumption that the growth and development of a child was quite linear. This is why traditional schools tend to divide children into grade levels according to their chronological age, increasing by one year at a time. However, Dr. Montessori extensively studied children with both the mind of a scientist and the heart of an educator, which led her to quite a different conclusion. She noted that children passed through what she called the four planes of development, more akin to a series of sequential growth "waves" than the traditionally held linear pattern. In each of these stages, or planes, a child initially experiences an explosion of growth that eventually plateaus and subsides. Each wave occurs over the course of six years, before the child finally moves into the next plane of development. Montessori schools group children into mixed-age classes containing a three-year age span, roughly corresponding to either the beginning or latter halves of the various planes of development.

The first plane of development—also the scope of this book—is **infancy**, which lasts from birth until age six. This is a period characterized by a child's need to attain physical and biological independence. Their efforts are focused on learning to coordinate their movements, communicate with others, and engage in purposeful work. It is a time of explosive growth, energetic activity, and strong emotions.

The first plane is also the period of **the absorbent mind**, when the child's mind is like a sponge, effortlessly absorbing a vast wealth of information about their environment, language, and culture. Based on her observations, Dr. Montessori further divided this plane into two subcategories: the *unconscious* absorbent mind (birth to three years) and the *conscious* absorbent mind (three to six years). Infants and toddlers are described as having an unconscious absorbent mind, as they primarily learn through their senses, without any conscious awareness or effort. For example, learning to walk and communicate through language are both accomplishments that the child achieves naturally and spontaneously. After the age of three, this learning becomes much more conscious on the child's part, as they begin to look for ways to organize their understanding of what was absorbed during the first three years. They learn with their hands and actively seek out experiences to aid in their intellectual development. During this time, it is quite common to hear a child emphatically wish to "do it myself."

The second plane of development is **childhood**, lasting from ages 6 to 12. This period is typified by the child's need to attain mental independence. It is a time of relative calm and stability, and children become developmentally ready to move from concrete to abstract learning. Children of this age are conceptual explorers, concerned with questions of justice, and use their imagination, abstract thought, and reasoning to develop their understanding of the world. They also become more interested in the value of social interaction with peers.

The third plane of development is **adolescence**, occurring from ages 12 to 18. This period is distinguished by a need to attain social and emotional independence. During this time, adolescents are concerned with the construction of their "social self" and are focused on developing their moral values. This plane is often compared to the first plane of development, as it is also marked by rapid change, emotional volatility, and sensitivity.

The fourth plane of development is **maturity**, which spans from ages 18 to 24. This period is marked by a need to attain spiritual, moral, and economic independence. During this time, young adults begin to pursue studies of personal interest that pertain to their ability to make a difference in the world, often deciding to further their education and/or choosing a career path. They actively work toward constructing an understanding of the self and endeavor to determine their place in society.

SENSITIVE PERIODS

Dr. Montessori also discovered that young children pass through several distinct stages of development that tend to occur at predictable ages. She referred to these windows of development as *sensitive periods*, which can be thought of as special times when your child's interests will be intensely focused on developing a particular skill or concept. It is also easiest for them to master a certain skill during this time.

Knowing when these sensitive periods occur can prepare you to look for signs of them in your child's interests and behaviors, at which point you can readily adapt the environment accordingly. The various sensitive periods are as follows:

- **Movement (birth–2.5 years):** Children work toward the mastery of their gross- and fine-motor control.

- **Language (birth–6 years):** Children begin acquiring the native language(s) of their environment through direct conversation and interactions with other people in real life, first receptively (what they understand others saying) and then expressively (their eventual speaking).

- **Order (6 months–4 years):** Children have an intense need for order in all aspects of life, from the organization of their physical environment to their daily rhythms at home.

- **Toilet learning (1–2.5 years):** Children begin showing an interest in the toilet and begin gaining better physical control over their own bodily functions.

- **Small objects (1–3.5 years):** Children become fixated on tiny objects and details in their environment, which helps develop their fine-motor control.

- **Refinement of the senses (2–6 years):** Children are deeply engaged by sensorial experiences related to taste, smell, sound, weight, and touch, which helps them classify objects in their environment.

- **Letter shapes and sounds (2.5–5 years):** Children are spontaneously interested in learning the shapes of letters and their corresponding sounds.

- **Grace and courtesy (2.5–6 years):** Children become interested and inclined toward social interactions with peers and the learning of manners.

- **Music (3 years+):** Children learn rhythm, pitch, melody, and other musical qualities; music helps develop the brain, leading to academic, social, and emotional growth.

- **Writing (3.5–4.5 years):** Once the child has mastered letter shapes and sounds, they begin putting letters together to "write" words using wooden alphabet letters.

- **Reading (4.5–5.5 years):** After the child is capable of writing and understanding their own words, they then move on to learning to read (the words of others).

- **Math (4–6 years):** Children are fascinated with numbers and quantities.

THE NEED FOR FREEDOM

From the time of birth, children also require **freedom of movement.** They have a developmental need to stretch their arms and legs, turn their heads, and explore the capabilities of their own bodies. This movement is essential to a child's development, and every effort must be made not to restrict a child's natural urge for such movements. This means that baby-holding devices should be avoided (perhaps with the exception of baby-wearing on occasion), and instead, your infant should be laid down on a soft blanket or mat on the floor to stretch, observe, and move about according to their natural inclinations. Toddlers and preschoolers also require freedom of movement as they walk, run, climb, take activities to and from their shelf, and engage in practical-life work.

You may also notice your young child exerting what Dr. Montessori called **maximum effort,** a natural tendency that motivates them to push their own physical capabilities to their absolute limit. Babies will expend great effort trying to grab a toy that's just out of reach or to figure out how to roll over for the first time, likely making lots of noises as they do. Toddlers and preschoolers like to walk great distances and push, pull, or carry very heavy loads. As the adult, you must respect these natural urges and not only resist the temptation to intervene but also find ways to create more opportunities for it.

Other critical needs of young children that are recognized in the Montessori approach (especially in the context of the home environment) are the **freedom of choice** and the **freedom of repetition.** Freedom of choice does not imply that children are free to do as they please; instead, they are respectfully trusted to make limited choices throughout each day. Some examples are selecting their own activity from the shelf (from what you've prepared), the outfit or shoes they'd like to wear (from two seasonally appropriate options), or the snack they'd like to have (from healthy options that you've made available).

Freedom of repetition simply means that a child is offered the opportunity to work on an activity at their own pace for as long as they'd like, sometimes even repeating the activity many times. At home, this freedom can be easily aided by not rushing your child to finish a task (and leaving more time for repetition), not rotating your child's toys too often, allowing your child to decide when they're done with their turn with a toy, and maintaining predictable family routines and rhythms that your child can learn to count on each day.

THE BEDROOM
SLEEP & RELAXATION

Sleep is a precious commodity for all children. When considering the design of an infant's nursery or young child's bedroom, the Montessori approach is rooted in one simple idea: the promotion of restful, restorative sleep on the child's terms. Unlike traditional nurseries, the goal is not to adorn the child's room with an excessive amount of decor, toys, and other distracting stimuli. Instead, the aim is to create beauty in simplicity.

A Montessori bedroom is typically quite minimal, exuding an atmosphere of peace and serenity. In order to avoid unnecessary visual clutter, the bedroom contains only the most essential furniture pieces. The color palette leans toward muted or neutral tones, although minor pops of color may also be found. Decor is minimal, usually including just a few pieces of high-quality artwork hung at the child's eye level and perhaps a small plant. A small selection of toys are offered on a low shelf that can be easily accessed during periods when the child is awake, just before sleeping, and upon waking up.

Aside from encouraging restful sleep, the child's bedroom is also designed to offer independence. This is why a traditional crib is not commonly used in a Montessori environment, since a child relies on an adult to help them into and out of it for sleeping. Instead, the child sleeps on a floor bed, which can be a simple mattress laid directly on the floor, or it can be placed in a low floor bed frame that enables the child to get in and out independently. We will discuss more about using a floor bed at various ages throughout this chapter.

Since a child is given the freedom to explore the room unsupervised, safety is of paramount importance. All furniture pieces must be securely mounted to the walls, electrical outlets should be covered, cords should be safely tucked away, and any decor items must either be completely safe for the child to explore or otherwise be stored out of reach.

Although these are the most common elements to consider, some aspects will necessarily change as a child grows. Let's take a closer look at how to set up an age-appropriate Montessori bedroom beginning in infancy and extending through toddlerhood and the preschool years.

INFANTS

THE FLOOR BED

In much of Western culture, a traditional crib is predominantly used for infant sleep, so the concept of an infant under the age of 12 months sleeping in a floor bed seems very strange and novel to most families who are new to Montessori. However, respect for our child's independence, even with regard to sleep, is of great importance from the moment of birth.

We must first realize that infants are not helpless and without thoughts or opinions. On the contrary, they are unique individuals who possess their own perspectives and experiences of the world. They should be offered the same basic freedoms as any other human being, provided that we are doing our part to keep them safe. A floor bed is used in a Montessori bedroom for the express purpose of respecting their independence and, although very young infants are initially quite immobile and cannot yet take advantage of it, they do grow very quickly. By three to four months old, babies are pushing up, rolling over, and beginning to actively explore the environment.

A great benefit of having your child use a floor bed for sleeping from the time of infancy is that there is never a "transition" period once they become toddlers. If the floor bed is all they have ever known, then it doesn't really ever come into question for them that there is any other option. It is just their "normal."

Setting up an infant floor bed is quite simple. All you need is a mattress and a tight fitted sheet. It's advisable to use a crib-sized mattress for safe sleep until your child is at least 12 months old, but some families will choose to start with a firm, innerspring twin-sized mattress from the beginning. (It makes night feedings a lot easier when a parent can lie down next to the baby and get up without disturbing the baby's sleep when finished.) Be sure to follow all guidelines for safe sleep: there should be no padding, pillow-top cover, memory foam, pillows, loose blankets, lovies, stuffed animals, or any other items in the bed with your baby.

Another option is to place the mattress in a simple floor bed frame to help promote proper airflow to the underside of the mattress. While a frame is certainly nice to have, it isn't a necessity as long as the mattress is propped up for a few hours on a regular basis (such as when changing the sheets) so it can air out.

These are some of the most common questions that parents of infants typically have about using a floor bed:

- **At what age should I begin allowing my baby to sleep in the floor bed?** This decision is a very personal one, and there is no single answer. Some families will actually start their newborns in a floor bed from day one, while others will use a bassinet until about four to six months old, when the baby is actively rolling and has officially outgrown the bassinet. You can also start out by using the floor bed for daytime naps only, and then eventually transition to the floor bed for nighttime sleep, too. What you ultimately decide will come down to what you are most comfortable with doing.

- **Won't my baby roll out of the bed?** Not every baby will do this, but it's certainly a possibility when they first begin learning the physical boundaries of the bed. If your baby is a particularly active sleeper,

they may continue to roll out of the bed for quite some time before learning to recognize the edges. The good news is that the fall is only a couple of inches onto a padded surface, so they will be none the worse for the wear. (And it is certainly much less dangerous than a baby who decides to climb over a crib railing.) Curiously, it isn't uncommon for infants who accidentally roll out of bed in their sleep to fall back to sleep right on the floor where they land. However, if they cry or otherwise call out for you, then it is advisable to go into the room to help them settle back into the bed for sleep.

- **What if my baby gets out of bed and falls asleep on the floor?** It happens, and that's okay! As long as your infant seems to be sleeping comfortably, there is no need to disturb them. If they wake on their own, they will sometimes move themselves back to the bed if they are mobile enough.

- **What if my baby gets out of bed and crawls to the door after I've left the room?** This is certainly a possible scenario, though not all babies will do this. If it happens, there's not much to worry about. Your infant will either go back to the bed after a little while once they become tired, or they will simply fall asleep on the floor right where they are. And as was mentioned previously, this is totally fine as long as they seem comfortable. Just be sure to open the door slowly and carefully when you finally re-enter the room in case your baby is very close to the other side of the door.

CHANGING AREA

An infant's changing area can be very simple: a dresser with a changing pad on top, a changing table, or even just a changing pad on the floor. Keep a caddy nearby containing only the basic diapering essentials (out of baby's reach when they are left for unsupervised sleep). Consider adding some high-quality artwork or high-contrast, black-and-white images to the wall adjacent to the changing area to help engage your baby's brain and visual sense during diaper changes.

CLOTHING STORAGE

Where and how you store your infant's clothing is up to you during the initial months when they are not quite as active in the process of dressing themselves each day (at least in the sense of being able to choose their own clothing). It's worth considering ahead of time, though, how you might make it possible to provide your baby with independent access to their clothing once they become a toddler (more on this in the next section). And as they grow closer to their first birthday, you can begin introducing them to the process by offering them a choice between two outfits that you've selected for them.

INFANT SHELF

Toys in your infant's room should be very limited. As we've already discussed, the goal is to promote sleep, not entertainment. Choose just a small selection of three to four simple toys to place on a low shelf that your infant can easily access during times when they are awake before or after sleeping.

BOOK BASKET

Reading with your infant is a fabulous way to both deepen your connection and promote language development. Keep a small basket (or bookshelf) containing just a few books somewhere near your child's activity shelf for reading together before bedtime and for your infant to independently access during waking times.

LOW WALL ARTWORK

Your infant is learning about the world from the moment that they are born, absorbing every bit of the environment through all of their senses. Select a few pieces of high-quality artwork (even classic masterpieces!) to display in your baby's room, down low, at their eye level. To safely mount artwork to the wall, you can print and laminate it, then secure it to the wall with sticky Command strips. Another possibility is to frame the artwork with either no glass at all or with shatterproof acrylic "glass," and then mount the frame to the wall using Command picture-hanging strips.

CAREGIVER'S CHAIR

During the months that your baby still wakes at night to feed, if you are not offering milk directly in your infant's bed, then you might also consider keeping a cozy chair or glider in the room for a parent to use. Just make sure that the chair is safe enough to be left unsupervised with a baby (nothing that can pinch fingers or easily tip over) and that the chair is removed from the room as soon as your baby becomes more mobile.

OPTIONAL ELEMENTS

Other things to consider including in your infant's room are a sound machine, room-darkening curtains, a dim nightlight, and a baby monitor. These items don't have any explicit ties to Montessori philosophy, but they are certainly Montessori friendly, and many parents find them to be helpful in promoting restful sleep for their little one.

TODDLERS

THE FLOOR BED

Toddlers have a developmental need for freedom and autonomy. However, they spend a majority of their day being told what, when, and how to do things by adults. Many of these decrees are fair and warranted for their own health and safety. But there are a few areas over which an adult does not have power: eating, toileting, and sleeping. Try as we might to struggle against this reality at times, the cards are squarely in our child's hands. We simply cannot force a child to eat, use the toilet, or sleep against their will (nor should we try).

Our children are natural experts at listening to their own bodies and we owe them the respect of at least providing them freedom within limits in these areas. Using a floor bed in your toddler's bedroom is an excellent way to communicate this understanding and respect for their needs. They are able to get in and out of their beds independently of their own will and can choose to sleep when they decide they are ready. (Guidelines for initially setting up and using a floor bed are discussed in the previous section on infant sleep.)

If you are newly transitioning a one- to two-year-old toddler to their own floor bed after previous time spent sleeping in a crib (or co-sleeping with a parent), there will likely be a short transition period as they become accustomed to the new arrangement. Many families find it helpful to have their toddler "practice" sleeping in the floor bed only for daytime naps initially, and as they become more comfortable, transition to using the floor bed for both naps and nighttime sleep. How long this transition period lasts is unique to the child, as some toddlers seem to accept the floor bed more readily than others. The best approach in any scenario is to express confidence in your toddler's ability to make the transition successfully.

Parents of toddlers often have some of the same questions as do the parents of infants. Be sure to read through those questions and answers in the previous section on infants, especially if your toddler is newly transitioning to the use of a floor bed. In addition, here are a few other common questions that tend to arise with toddlers specifically:

- **Won't my child get out of bed?** Yes, especially in the beginning when it is still new. This is normal and to be expected as your toddler explores their newfound freedom. Once the novelty wears off, toddlers most often tend to remain in bed.

- **What if my child plays all night instead of sleeping?** Possible? Yes. But this is not quite as likely as you might imagine. Toddlers who decide to play before sleeping will typically play for a brief amount of time until they begin to truly feel tired and naturally fall asleep. Again, we must have faith that our children can effectively respond to their own biological cues!

- **What if my child leaves the room?** This may happen in the early stages of using a floor bed, although it wanes over time. If your child leaves the room, the most effective approach is to gently, kindly, and confidently lead your child back to the bed, tuck them in again, and leave. It is best to do this as quietly as possible, without much conversation. If safety upon leaving the bedroom is a concern, simply close the door all the way or place a pressure-mounted safety gate in the door frame to ensure that your child will not be able to leave the room unsupervised.

CARE-OF-SELF AREA

When your infant becomes a toddler, the need for nighttime diaper changes should be much less frequent, at which point the changing area should be relocated to the bathroom. This is to begin creating toilet awareness for your child so they learn to associate bodily functions with the natural place in your home where toileting should occur. In lieu of the changing area in your child's room, you will likely have some extra space for the creation of a simple care-of-self area. This area could include a low mirror, a small shelf for a brush or other care items, and a small stool or chair for your child to sit on as they learn to dress themselves.

ACCESS TO CLOTHING

Providing easy access to their own clothing is an essential step toward your toddler's developing ability to dress independently. This can be accomplished in several ways, based on your existing space and budget. Potential ideas include the use of baskets for each type of clothing (e.g., shirts, pants, socks, underwear, etc.) that are stored at your child's level, adding a child-height clothing rod to an existing closet for hanging clothes, a dresser with low drawers that are dedicated exclusively to your child's clothing, or even a full child-sized wardrobe.

In the beginning, you can help your toddler choose from two different choices of each clothing item (or complete outfits) that you've preselected for them. However, as they grow older, your child may want to choose their own clothing each day from the entire available selection, so be sure to only provide a limited number of seasonally appropriate choices and store any out-of-season clothing elsewhere.

Know that your toddler may also go through a short exploratory phase in the beginning where they pull clothing out of the baskets, closet, or drawers during unsupervised times. This is totally normal! The most effective response is to matter-of-factly point out what has happened, remind them that their clothing should stay in the baskets or drawers, and invite them to assist you in putting things away again.

TODDLER SHELF

When it comes to toys, it is a wise idea to keep things simple in your toddler's bedroom. Recall that your goal isn't to provide hours of entertainment but rather to create a restful space that invites sleep. So just as you did when they were an infant, stick to providing a small selection of three to four simple toys that can be freely accessed during independent play, usually before going to sleep or when they first wake up. Rotate the toys periodically to help maintain your child's interest.

READING AREA

You can also set up a small corner of your toddler's bedroom that is dedicated to reading. It doesn't need to be fancy—just a small basket or shelf of books, along with a comfy rug or chair, is perfect. If you want to up the cozy factor, you can add a soft blanket and a pillow or two.

LOW WALL ARTWORK

Your toddler may appreciate a change of scenery from their baby days, so feel free to add (or switch up) some high-quality artwork in their bedroom. Think outside the box— stunning landscapes, plant and animal photography, abstract works, and even classic masterpieces! Be sure to mount it down low on the wall where they can see it. You can do this either by printing and laminating the artwork and then securing to the wall with sticky Command strips or by framing the artwork and using Command picture-hanging strips and acrylic "glass" (or no glass at all) for safety.

LIGHT SWITCH

It is also a boon to your toddler's independence to have access to the light switch in their bedroom so they can turn the light on by themselves if they need to. You can do this by simply adding a light switch extender. If this isn't an option due to the type of light switch you have or if there isn't a light already installed in your child's bedroom, then a great alternative is to install a smart bulb in a small table lamp. This type of bulb connects wirelessly to an included remote, which you can easily mount on the wall at your child's level.

PRESCHOOLERS

FLOOR OR RAISED BED

By the time your child is a preschooler, they are likely to be quite comfortable sleeping in their Montessori floor bed. (Guidance on the setup and use of a floor bed can be found in both of the previous sections of this chapter.)

If your child wants to continue sleeping in a floor bed, there is no need to change anything. Do not feel pressured to move your child into a regular raised bed (off the floor) just because they are older. Simply follow their lead until they are ready!

ACCESS TO CLOTHING

Not only can your preschooler independently dress themselves by now, but they will also most likely want to choose their own outfit each day. Thus, having easy access to their clothing is an absolute must. If you have not yet created a system for storing your child's clothing that allows them to choose what they'd like on their own, then now is definitely the time to do it. (For easy setup ideas, review this area in the previous "Toddlers" section.)

CARE-OF-SELF AREA

The care-of-self area will likely not have changed much from your child's toddler years: it will still include a mirror, low shelf for a hairbrush, and possibly a small stool or chair. One possible addition might be to provide access to a small basket of accessories or any other care essentials that your child frequently uses during their morning and bedtime routines.

PRESCHOOLER SHELF

Since your preschooler still needs a lot of sleep to support their rapidly growing brain, they shouldn't have many toys available in the room at any given time—just three to four options are still going to be more than enough. It is better to keep the majority of the available rotation of toys in their primary play space and store most other toys and activities out of reach. (Note: If due to the layout of your home your child's primary play space must be located in their bedroom, then toy rotation will be essential in minimizing the potential for clutter in your child's bedroom.) There is also a good chance that your preschooler will have some favorite toys or other special items that they need to have a dedicated place for storing when not in use, and the shelf in their bedroom is the perfect spot for these kinds of items. (This is especially helpful if there are younger siblings with curious little fingers!)

READING AREA

Your child's interest in books is likely exploding at this age, so offering a cozy little reading nook in their bedroom is essential. Do this by setting up one corner with a comfy rug, a chair, and a small bookshelf to house some of your child's favorite titles. Your preschooler is likely to use this space more often for independent reading than when they were a toddler, so feel free to make the space appealing by adding a few pillows, a blanket, and maybe even a small teepee tent.

LOW WALL ARTWORK

Preschool children will greatly appreciate being offered a choice in the artwork displayed in their bedroom—after all, they're the ones who have to look at it every day and night! Have a conversation with your child about what kinds of art they like, which will very likely be based on their interests at this age (e.g., animals, flowers, trains, outer space, etc.). Then conduct your own research to find several options from which they can choose. Mount your child's final selections at their eye level, either by printing and laminating the artwork and then securing it to the wall with Command strips or by framing the artwork and using Command picture-hanging strips and acrylic "glass" (or no glass at all) for safety.

LIGHT SWITCH

Your preschooler may finally be tall enough to reach the light switch on their own, negating the need for an extender. However, if there isn't a light already installed in your child's bedroom, then it is recommended to find a way to provide a source of light, since preschool-aged children have a genuine need to use their bedroom light at times (e.g., during independent reading or play in the early morning or before bedtime). An easy idea is to install a smart bulb in a small table lamp, which connects wirelessly to an included remote that can be mounted on the wall at your child's level.

THE BATHROOM
CARE OF SELF

One of the greatest gifts that can be offered to our children in the midst of their quest for independence is that of learning how to competently care for their own bodies, an area of practical life often referred to as *care of self*.

Dressing, brushing teeth, combing hair, bathing, toileting—all of these things amount to a daily checklist that we are primarily focused on checking off as quickly as possible. As busy adults with jam-packed agendas and schedules, we often find ourselves in a rush to simply get the job done, without stopping to consider how much our children are actually capable of doing on their own. Yet, even infants are capable of contributing to these seemingly mundane tasks of life in small ways, if only we could alter our mindsets to see these routines through their eyes.

Young babies can easily push their foot through a pant leg during a diaper change, while older babies can begin standing up during diaper changes to more fully participate in the process. Toddlers will enthusiastically dive into learning how to properly wash their own hands and, in a thoughtfully prepared space, can even successfully use the toilet. And so long as they have had adequate practice and are provided with access to what they need, preschoolers can be fully independent in getting themselves ready for school each morning.

We are our child's first guide in learning what it means to be human, and this includes the basic dignities of good health and proper hygiene. Although it may take some conscious effort on our part, it is our ultimate responsibility to slow down and offer an environment that affords our child the freedom they require to learn how to care for themselves.

In this chapter, we'll focus on how to properly prepare the bathroom environment in order to guide your child toward active participation and functional independence in the care of their bodies.

INFANTS

When your child is a newborn and you're still in survival mode, diaper changes are going to take place in a multitude of interesting places. While you may very well have set up a designated changing area for your baby, you may also find that the bed, couch, floor, or even the front seat of your car is just *way* more convenient in the heat of the moment. In the first few weeks and months of your child's life, the general rule of thumb is that you simply *do what you need to do.*

However, once you find yourself falling into a more predictable rhythm with your infant, it's likely that diaper changes will more often begin taking place in a specific, designated space. The changing area might be located in either your bedroom or your child's bedroom, but it might also exist in another area of your home where your baby spends a lot of time.

As your child becomes interested in learning to roll over, you may find it easier and safer to change them on a light blanket or changing pad placed directly on the floor. But once your baby can pull up on furniture to a steady standing position (and sometimes even sooner), you'll likely discover that they are no longer interested in lying down for diaper changes. They will do everything in their power to wriggle away from you—not with the intent of being "naughty," as you might think—but because they have an intense developmental urge to both achieve an upright posture and exert their growing independence.

When this happens, save yourself unnecessary frustration by resisting the urge to force your child to lie down, and instead lean into your child's natural urges by calmly introducing a new way to do things. Make the switch to changing your child's diaper while they stand. (They can hold onto a nearby sturdy piece of furniture for added stability, if necessary.) Not only does this make the whole process a lot easier for you, as your child will be much more cooperative, but it is also a much more respectful approach that takes your child's developing needs into consideration. If your child is interested, you can also invite them to retrieve a clean diaper or wipes from wherever they are stored, undo the diaper tabs on their own, and discard the soiled diaper in the appropriate location once you're finished.

The time during which your infant begins crawling and eventually pulling up to stand is often also a good time to move the primary changing area to the bathroom of your home. The reason for this is to begin creating "toilet awareness." In doing so, you are helping your child begin to associate their bodily functions related to toileting with the natural area in your home where they should occur. And as your child moves into toddlerhood, this will facilitate the actual process of toilet learning, as they will already possess an experiential understanding of this concept.

Finally, as in all of your other interactions, it is respectful to make eye contact and gently talk to your infant about what you're doing whenever you must manipulate their body in some way. During diaper changes this might sound like: "I'm going to lift your legs . . . and now I'm going to wipe your bottom." Or "It's time to take off your diaper. Would you like to open the tabs?" During bath time: "I'm going to pour water onto your hair . . . and now I'm going to add some soap. Okay, I'm going to rinse your hair again."

It might feel silly when you first begin narrating these mundane tasks out loud to your infant, as they won't verbally respond to you like an older child would. But always remember that our babies understand much more than they can express, and they will appreciate an invitation from us to participate in these tasks in whatever capacity they are able. In any situation, we must treat them with the same level of gentle respect and courtesy that we would ourselves appreciate if we were less able-bodied and in the care of another person.

TODDLERS

As your infant moves into the toddler years, they will become quite eager to have more independence in completing many of the care tasks that you have been assisting them with thus far. A toddler's greatest request is this: "Help me to help myself!" Often, your child will even tell you this flat out: "Me do it!" This is a big developmental milestone in your child's life and one that marks a major step forward in their process of individuating themselves from you. They *want* to be allowed to do things for themselves.

Your role is simply to demonstrate a task and then step back to allow your child the freedom to learn and practice in their own way. Sit on your hands, bite your tongue, do whatever you need to do to 100 percent give them the reins. You will, of course, still remain present for safety purposes and to help but only if your child asks for your help. Otherwise, your primary job is to respect your child's efforts without interfering.

ACCESS TO WATER AND TOILETRIES

In the bathroom, a toddler who has learned to climb will appreciate having a sturdy two-tier step stool to help them to reach the height of the sink. In this way, they are able to freely use the sink for any care-of-self tasks that may require access to water, such as hand washing or teeth brushing. It is also helpful to have a mirror in the same area so your child can see their reflection as they complete these tasks. Also consider how you can provide your toddler with easy, independent access to their personal care essentials: toothbrush, toothpaste, cup, hairbrush, nailbrush, and any other items they use. A low drawer or small basket placed within reach is usually sufficient.

HANDWASHING

An alternative to consider is the addition of a small Montessori handwashing station. This can be purchased as a standalone unit (see "Montessori Furniture & Materials"), or you can DIY using a large bowl, pitcher, soap, and hand towel arranged on a low table or shelf. Since it is located at your toddler's natural height, they can learn to wash their hands and perform other care-of-self tasks with great ease.

To use the handwashing station, your toddler first learns to fill the basin with an ample amount of water, either using a pitcher or water dispenser, depending on your setup. Then they lightly wet their hands in the water and add soap (usually a travel-sized bar or a liquid pump that they are able to operate). They spend a minute or two washing their hands thoroughly—being sure to wash the

tops of hands, palms, and between fingers—followed by rinsing their hands in the water basin and using the hand towel to dry their hands. Finally, they empty the dirty water basin into the designated place, such as a sink or bucket, and put it back in the station. They can also use a separate towel to dry any accidental splashes or spills.

And if a small mirror and basket for essentials are added to the station, then your toddler can use this area for all of their typical care-of-self tasks.

CLEANING FINGERNAILS

Your toddler may also appreciate being offered a small nailbrush to allow them to clean underneath their fingernails. This can be done as a part of their daily routine or on an as-needed basis. Demonstrate for your child how to use the nailbrush the first time and then allow them to practice on their own.

TOOTHBRUSHING

For many parents, brushing their toddler's teeth is a task that invites struggle, but it doesn't have to be this way. Providing your child with access to their own toothbrush and toothpaste and showing them how to complete this task on their own will go a long way to avoiding a battle. To keep things fun and provide good modeling, invent a fun toothbrushing song or consider brushing your own teeth alongside your toddler. And to ensure that their teeth are adequately clean, simply make a habit of taking turns: "Your turn to brush first! . . . Okay, now it's Mama's turn to brush your teeth!"

BATHING

When it comes to bath time, you can offer your toddler more independence by providing a travel-sized shampoo bottle that they can use on their own, as well as a washcloth or travel-sized loofah. Allow your child to squeeze the soap, if they'd like and have their turn washing first, followed by your turn to make sure their hair and body are adequately clean. Don't forget to gently let your child know what you're doing: "Okay, I'm going to pour water over your hair now. . . . Can you lean your head back?"

TOILET LEARNING

Once toddlers are independently walking, they may also be ready to begin the toilet-learning process. This isn't something that happens overnight, in three days, or even in a week. It also doesn't require rewards or punishments. Rather, it's a slow, gradual process that respects your child's growing awareness, interest, and abilities; and it may take weeks or even months. Resist the temptation to rush your child through this natural human experience, and focus on following their lead.

To begin preparing the environment, place a small potty seat in the bathroom, along with a basket of essentials, such as clean underwear and toilet paper (or wipes). Allow your toddler to sit on it whenever they'd like to help normalize its use. You can also use a seat reducer and step stool for a regular-sized toilet, but some toddlers may feel safer and have more success in independently using a small potty seat.

Put your toddler in cotton training underwear during the daytime so that they can begin to associate the sensation of wetness with their bodily functions. Offer the potty at regular times (e.g., during diaper changes or before and after naps, meals, and car trips), but don't insist on it. Always respect your child's readiness. And when your child does have

success, resist the urge to overpraise and cheer. Your child's motivation and sense of accomplishment in using the toilet should always remain intrinsic.

When accidents happen, avoid shaming your toddler. Treat the situation casually, without judgment, and involve your child in helping to clean up as best as they can: "Uh oh, it looks like your pants are wet. Let's get you into some dry pants. . . . Now let's wipe this up. . . . Would you please put your wet pants into the dirty laundry basket? Thank you!"

Over time, your toddler will begin to recognize their own bodily urges before they happen, and accidents will become much less frequent. All children are different: some will let you know that they need to use the toilet, in which case you can assist them, while others will be happy to take themselves to the toilet.

Although accidents and extra laundry are inconvenient, always try to remain positive and respectful of your child's progress, however long it may take. Learning to independently use the toilet is something that all children will eventually master, and we must maintain confidence in our children's ability to be independently successful.

PRESCHOOLERS

ACHIEVING INDEPENDENCE

With the proper environment and sufficient freedom to develop their skills, a neurotypical preschool-aged child is capable of achieving a basic level of functional independence. A parent should, of course, still remain on standby in the event that the child requests assistance, which is likely to happen on days when the child may be feeling ill; is experiencing a major change in their normal routines, such as the birth of a sibling, divorce, or moving to a new home; or is simply having an off day.

This is not to say that a three- or four-year-old should be left to brush their teeth and bathe themselves alone. On the contrary, you should still remain present for general supervision and safety (especially with regard to baths). But for the most part, your role will shift primarily to smaller check-ins with your child on the specific tasks they are completing.

For example, your preschooler can easily choose their own outfit for the day from their wardrobe and dress themselves independently,

while you might just check in to make sure they are fully dressed before leaving the house. (No, matching should not be a concern.) Your preschooler can also brush their own teeth, with an extra little scrub from you right before they finish. They should also be able to comb their own hair, use the toilet independently (with some assistance in wiping at times), and wash their own hair and bodies at bath time (with your help in rinsing, if necessary).

Keep in mind, though, that these capabilities are not entirely age dependent; just because a child is four years old does not automatically imply that they will be able to do all of these things with ease. Their actual level of independence is going to heavily rely on their previous experience with care-of-self tasks. Thus, if you are offering the responsibility for completing these tasks to an older child for the very first time, realize that they will likely require some time for catching up a bit before finally finding success.

Instead of being hyperfocused on what your child cannot yet do, try to shift your mindset to one of respecting your child's unique timetable

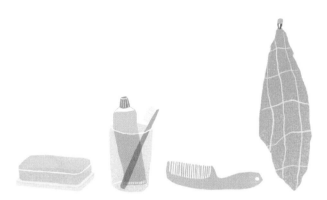

by meeting them exactly where they're at. Then you can begin gradually shifting more of the responsibility to your child as you observe their level of skill improving.

For example, a child who is accustomed to a parent dressing them each morning before school is likely to have difficulty in getting dressed all by themselves right away. They may even actively resist, as it's much more convenient to just let someone do everything for you. But you can help your child learn to get dressed independently over time by first inviting them to choose their outfit without your input. Then you can encourage them to put on their own undergarments while you do the rest. Eventually, they can be responsible for undergarments, shirt, and pants, until finally they are putting on an entire outfit by themselves, even without you in the room.

A NOTE ON PRIVACY

Although your child may not have had a sense of privacy as an infant or toddler, you may begin to notice that your preschooler actively seeks out privacy at certain times. It may only happen during certain care-of-self tasks,

such as getting dressed or using the toilet, and it may not be every time but rather only on random occasions.

If your child shuts a door or otherwise requests privacy, do your best to respect their wishes, with the only exception being a potential safety concern. It is likely that your child has seen this being modeled in your home by adults or older children, and they may simply be experimenting with the powerful feeling of being able to shut a door to keep others (even the grown-ups!) out of a room. As always, we must remind ourselves that children are small human beings, deserving of as much respect as we might offer another adult. So if they express a need for privacy, we should step back and allow for it. (And if we need to enter, respectfully knock and ask their permission instead of barging in.) This is a normal progression for all children as they begin to individuate themselves from the adults in their lives, and our role is to avoid interfering with this natural order of development.

THE ENTRYWAY
LEAVING & RETURNING HOME

Many parents find themselves stressed by the idea of having to get their child ready to leave the house because it has turned into a battleground of sorts. Much time and energy is often wasted in trying to coax a child into finding their shoes and putting them on or retrieving their coat and then staying still long enough for the parent to hastily put it on for them. Or perhaps the child's backpack or some other important accessory is always conveniently missing when it's time to go, which then adds an exasperating extra 10 minutes of hunting around the house for it.

Here's some good news: it doesn't have to be this way. Setting up our homes in ways that show respect for our children's capabilities means intentionally creating functional spaces that are designed for their everyday use. And this includes even the smaller, oft-forgotten areas like the entryway.

If you take a moment to think about it, we must leave and return to our homes many times throughout the week for work, school, errands, or even just daily playtime outside. Keeping this in mind, it might be easier to see how the entryway serves as a critical space in which we can easily offer our children a multitude of opportunities for independence. And taking the time to consider how we can better meet our child's needs in this area of our home will ultimately make the task of coming and going a lot easier and more enjoyable for everyone involved.

In this chapter, we'll discuss ideas for preparing a functional entryway that encourages your child to take real ownership of, and pride in, the tasks required for leaving and returning home each day.

SETTING UP THE ENTRYWAY

Our children often find themselves at odds with a traditional home environment, as the physical space is usually designed with adult proportions in mind. Thought isn't always given to the needs of our smallest family members, who are too short to reach much of anything without the assistance of an adult. And as you can imagine, this can feel quite frustrating for the young child who wants (and needs!) to be able to do things on their own.

One of the many ways we can show respect for our child is in offering them the same common courtesies that we typically enjoy as adults. We wouldn't hang hooks so high on the wall that we must get on tippy-toe to reach for our coat, nor would we particularly enjoy sitting on the floor to get on our shoes every time. We also might find it irritating if we can't find our favorite pair of sunglasses or if we have to go hunting for our car keys that seem to have been misplaced (yet again).

It's easier to make changes to your child's environment that will better suit their needs when you're able to truly see the space from their perspective. So get down on your hands and knees in the entryway of your home and look around. What do you see that's too high and out of your child's reach? Is there a designated place for all of the things your child needs—shoes, coat, backpack, weather accessories—and are these places easily accessible to your child? Is there a comfortable place to sit while they put on their shoes?

Here are some easy-to-implement ideas to consider as you transform the entryway of your home into a more child-friendly space:

- **Low wall hooks:** Install one or two hooks low on the wall, at your child's height, where they can independently hang their coat and/or a backpack. If your child has multiple coats, then be sure to limit the available options to just two acceptable choices. (Pro tip: if you use hooks that adhere to the wall using 3M Command strips, then you'll be able to easily readjust their placement as your child grows taller without damaging the wall.)

- **Shoe storage:** Add a small basket or low shelf for your child to neatly store their shoes. To avoid power struggles over choice of footwear, only keep seasonally appropriate options stored in this area (i.e., no flip-flops in wintertime), and limit the available options to just two.

- **A basket for accessories:** If your child has need of any accessories for various weather conditions (such as gloves, sunglasses, a hat, or an umbrella), store these in their own special basket located near everything else. Again, be sure these items are seasonally appropriate. Depending on your setup, the basket can be wall-mounted at your child's height or placed on a low shelf that your child can easily access.

- **A place to sit:** Provide a comfortable place for your child to sit as they put on their shoes by adding a child-sized chair, small wooden stool, or low bench. Alternatively, if you happen to have a staircase in your home that is located close to the door, then it might also be easy enough for your child to use the bottom step for seating.

INVITING COOPERATION

Aside from preparing the physical environment, we must also consider the tone and nature of our interactions with our child. Are we taking over and rushing them through these tasks, or are we slowing down and allowing them to take the lead (while we remain on standby for assistance)? Here are a few simple guidelines to keep in mind:

- It is much easier to remain patient and calm when you aren't feeling like you're going to be late, so do your best to **build a few extra minutes into your daily schedule** so that your child is able to move at their own pace.

- **Offer limited choices** as your child moves through the tasks of getting ready. For example: "Would you like to wear the blue coat or the green coat?" Or "Would you like to put on your shoes by yourself, or would you like me to help you?"

- Instead of making threatening statements, such as "Put on your shoes right now, or we are *not* going to the park!", try to **describe the situation neutrally:** "As soon as you put on your shoes, then we can go to the park." If your child chooses not to put on their shoes (but will also not accept help from you), then the simple and natural consequence is that they won't be able to go to the park that day.

If your child actively resists leaving the house, respect and acknowledge their feelings with genuine empathy: "You aren't ready to go to school today. I hear you. (*Pause.*) Here are your shoes. Would you like me to help you put them on?" (And if they continue to resist, then move on with helping them to get ready, even as you continue to patiently and gently acknowledge their feelings about what's happening: "It looks like you need some help, so I'm going to put your shoes on for you. . . . You don't like that I'm putting your shoes on. . . . I understand this is frustrating for you.")

THE KITCHEN
FOOD PREPARATION

Young children feel valued and empowered when they are able to contribute to the well-being of the family and home environment, and there is no better way to involve them than by inviting them into the kitchen to help with cooking and baking. This area of practical life is a cornerstone of many Montessori homes because it fills children with a sense of purpose as they work, fosters deep concentration, teaches life skills, and creates fond childhood memories.

Children are usually quite curious about what we're doing in the kitchen as we chop vegetables at the counter, mix ingredients together, or stir a pot on the stove. And dinnertime is often an understandably stressful time of day for many parents, as they find their children constantly requesting to be picked up or paid attention to in some way while they are trying to cook. However, when our children are instead offered the opportunity to work *alongside* us as we prepare meals, it often becomes a favorite time of day that both parents and children can look forward to.

And it should come as no surprise that children love to be involved with baking and cooking! The process itself is an exciting multisensory experience, with a great variety of colors, smells, sounds, textures, and tastes involved. By simply offering a safe stool to properly reach the height of the counter, as well as their own child-sized tools to work with, children will enthusiastically dive into learning how to prepare food, cook, and bake in whatever capacity they can. Children are also more apt to try new foods that they have personally helped to prepare in some way, which is certainly a bonus win for any parent!

In this chapter, we'll explore how to create a space in the kitchen that not only fosters your child's developmental needs, but which also invites their eager participation in the preparation of snacks and family meals.

INFANTS

It is critical to include our children in the ebb and flow of our homes from the first few days of life, as we go about our usual business of cleaning, cooking, and spending time together as a family. And although newborns and young infants are not yet capable of directly participating in the kitchen, there is something to be said about providing them with the opportunity to observe.

Newborns crave the warmth and security of being carried in arms or snuggled against the chest of a parent while in a baby carrier, during which time the parent may also be attending to house chores or engaging in conversation with other adults and children in the home. Meanwhile, the absorbent mind of the newborn child is taking in every bit of sensory input that is available. So if a parent or caregiver is holding (or wearing) the baby while also preparing a snack for an older sibling or cooking a family meal, then the newborn is also immersed in everything that's going on: the sights, smells, and sounds of the kitchen environment. If it is not possible to hold or wear your infant while working in the kitchen, you can always lay them down nearby on a cozy floor mat or blanket, where it is still possible for them to observe what's happening.

In either scenario, your baby is not only directly included in family life but is also indirectly absorbing various aspects of the kitchen-related tasks they will eventually be able to carry out by themselves when they grow older.

Once your infant is older and becomes more mobile, they can participate in the kitchen in a variety of different ways. Not only are they able to more directly observe while a parent is cooking if they are being held or worn in a carrier, but they may also be able to add large ingredient pieces (such as frozen fruit chunks for a smoothie) to a bowl or blender one at a time with assistance. They are also usually fairly enthusiastic taste-testers once they are eating solid foods. Older infants are also quite content to investigate the kitchen cabinets as they experiment with storage containers, nesting bowls, measuring cups, wooden kitchen utensils, and pots and pans while a parent cooks nearby.

TODDLERS

As your child becomes capable of walking independently, their hands are finally freed to engage in more purposeful work. In addition, they spent an entire year observing everything there is to know about daily life in your home. So by the time toddlerhood arrives, they are primed and eager to actively participate.

While inviting your child to help in the kitchen is an essential first step, there are also several aspects to consider when preparing the environment to truly make their participation and independence possible. There is a list of suggestions on where to find child-sized tools and furniture in the "Montessori Furniture & Materials" section, but keep in mind that it is entirely possible to repurpose tools and resources that you already have on hand. Children are resilient and will manage with whatever tools you have available.

ACCESS TO KITCHEN TOOLS AND SERVEWARE

Depending on the setup of your home, you may be able to utilize an existing low cabinet or drawer for storing your child's own small kitchen tools (e.g., cutting board, rolling pin, wavy chopper or nylon chef's knife, manual juicer, egg slicer, etc.) and a child-sized cooking apron, as well as utensils, plates, bowls, cups, and a placemat for mealtimes. Otherwise, you might consider adding a small shelf or cabinet located in or near the kitchen that your child can independently access. Be sure to organize items such that they are uncluttered and easy to find.

THE LEARNING TOWER

One of the greatest challenges that children face when working in the kitchen is not being able to reach the countertop. And while this problem could be easily solved with a sturdy step stool, oftentimes the stool isn't high enough to allow a child to comfortably work at countertop height. In addition, toddlers are not yet very stable or sure-footed and could easily take an accidental step off the edge of the stool they're standing on.

So what's a parent to do? Enter the learning tower, which is essentially a large step stool with safety rails surrounding all four sides.

The internet abounds with a variety of DIY tutorials for crafting a learning tower from scratch or hacking one from existing stools sold by various manufacturers. However, if the DIY route isn't your cup of tea, a learning tower can also be easily purchased from a variety of online retailers. And while the cost of a learning tower can be on the higher end of any expenses you might encounter in the name of setting up your home for your child's independence, most Montessori families will agree that it is quite arguably one of the most worthwhile investments.

The learning tower easily serves a number of functions for your growing toddler. Not only can they safely reach the countertop to observe, make their own snacks, and assist in preparing food for a family meal, but the placement of the learning tower in the kitchen also provides a convenient place to engage in messier practical-life or sensory activities, such as making playdough, oobleck, or anything involving water. You may also discover that your child prefers to eat small snacks while standing on the learning tower and will also use it to participate in other activities that you might find yourself doing in the kitchen, such as opening the mail.

INDEPENDENT SNACK SELECTION

One final aspect of the physical kitchen space is to consider how you can provide your child with the ability to choose their own snacks. For most families, this is usually an existing low cabinet, drawer, or basket that is periodically restocked by a parent with a limited number of healthy choices that the child can access independently. It can be helpful to have one specific place for dry goods that can be kept at room temperature (e.g., crackers or dried fruit) and a different place on a low shelf in the refrigerator for any items that must be kept cold (e.g., cheese, yogurt, or fresh produce).

An approach that some families take is to only place the maximum allowed number of snacks for the entire day in the snack storage area, and then allow their child to freely choose when they would like to have snacks throughout the day. If the child consumes all of their snacks very early in the day, then no more are provided (until the next day when it is restocked). Meanwhile, other families may be more comfortable with deciding on designated snack times throughout the day. How often you allow your child to have snacks will be a personal decision based on your family's own food culture.

RECIPES FOR TODDLERS

BERRY SUNRISE SMOOTHIE

YIELD: 2 (8oz; 240ml) smoothies

½ cup frozen berries
½ cup frozen mango (or pineapple) chunks
1 fresh, peeled mandarin orange
½ cup packed fresh baby spinach leaves
1½ cups water

Adult Prep: Premeasure all ingredients into several small ramekins, and place them on the table or countertop for your child. (You can invite your toddler to peel the mandarin orange on their own if they are able to do so. Otherwise, you can do this step for them.)

1. Invite your toddler to place all of the ingredients into a blender at their own pace, either by pouring the ingredients from the ramekins or by dropping the ingredients in by hand (depending on their level of skill).

2. Place the lid on the blender, and then invite your toddler to start it by using the appropriate button or knob. (You may need to assist during this step.) Blend until smooth.

3. Pour the smoothie into a small glass for your toddler. Invite them to place their own small drinking straw into the glass. (Cut the straw in half or thirds, depending on the height of the glass.)

AVOCADO TOAST & EGG

YIELD: 1 slice avocado toast + 1 hard-boiled egg

1 slice of bread
½ ripe avocado
1 hard-boiled egg (in shell)

Adult Prep: Make the hard-boiled egg ahead of time. When ready to make the recipe, peel and slice the avocado in half and place into a small ramekin. Gather all ingredients and tools, and place them on the table or countertop for your child.

1. With your supervision, invite your toddler to begin by toasting their slice of bread. Once the toast is cool, your toddler can transfer it to a child-sized plate.

2. Encourage your toddler to mash the avocado in the ramekin with a child-sized masher or small fork until a spreadable consistency is achieved. (You may need to assist with this step at times, until your toddler becomes more proficient.)

3. Invite your toddler to use a child-sized spreading knife to spread the mashed avocado onto their slice of toast. (Their final product will be a bit messy and imperfect, and that's okay!)

4. Once the avocado toast is complete, your toddler can peel the hard-boiled egg, placing the egg shells into a second ramekin (to be discarded).

5. Finally, your toddler can use an egg slicer to slice the peeled egg, and then transfer the egg slices to the plate (or on top of the toast, if desired).

BLACK BEAN QUESADILLAS

YIELD: 1 half-circle–sized quesadilla

1 flour tortilla

½ cup shredded Mexican cheese

¼ cup cooked black beans

Seasoning of choice (cumin, taco seasoning, etc.)

Cooking oil spray

Adult Prep: Premeasure the shredded cheese and black beans into two separate ramekins for your toddler. Place the tortilla on a large plate. Put everything together on the table or counter for your child. Lightly grease a medium pan with cooking spray.

1. Invite your toddler to sprinkle the black beans over one half of the tortilla, and then sprinkle the cheese over top of it. Finish by adding a light dusting of their seasoning of choice. (You will need to help with this part until your toddler is able to do it without overseasoning.)

2. Assist your toddler in gently folding the tortilla in half to make a half circle.

3. *Adult Only:* Heat the pan over medium heat, and cook the tortilla until lightly browned. Flip and cook the other side until also lightly browned. Transfer the quesadilla to a large plate or cutting board, and allow to cool slightly. Slice the quesadilla into four triangle-shaped wedges.

4. Your toddler can serve themselves their desired number of wedges onto their own child-sized plate.

OATMEAL CHOCOLATE CHIP COOKIES

YIELD: 12 cookies

½ cup butter, softened

½ cup packed brown sugar

½ cup white sugar

1 egg

½ tsp vanilla extract

2 tbsp quick-cooking oats

2 tbsp all-purpose flour

½ tsp baking soda

½ tsp baking powder

½ tsp salt

1 cup chocolate chips

Adult Prep: Preheat the oven to 350°F (175°C). Lightly grease a baking sheet. Premeasure all ingredients into small ramekins. Place everything on the table or countertop for your child.

1. Invite your toddler to add the butter, sugars, egg, and vanilla to a mixing bowl, and then stir everything together with a child-sized wooden spoon for about 5 minutes. (You may need to assist with this step.)

2. In another bowl, your toddler can add the oats, flour, baking soda, baking powder, and salt, and then stir everything together.

3. Invite your toddler to pour the wet ingredients into the dry ingredients, and stir again to combine everything.

4. Your toddler can then pour the ramekin of chocolate chips into the dough mixture, and stir to incorporate all ingredients.

5. Invite your toddler to use a spoon to scoop spoonfuls of cookie dough onto the greased baking sheet.

6. *Adult Only:* Bake cookies for 12 to 14 minutes. Allow to cool on the baking sheet for a few minutes before transferring to a wire rack.

PRESCHOOLERS

By the time a child is three to four years old, they are much more capable of performing a wide variety of kitchen-related tasks. While toddlers need ingredients measured for them ahead of time, a preschooler will actually want to learn how to use measuring cups and spoons to measure out ingredients for themselves. They also have greater strength and refined motor skills that enable them to use more specific kitchen tools on their own, such as a melon baller, rolling pin, cheese grater, apple slicer, mortar and pestle, and cookie cutters. With adult supervision, preschoolers can also learn how to safely use a child-sized knife, a Y-shaped peeler, and various kitchen appliances, such as a toaster. Once your child can reliably follow safety rules, they can also be introduced to cooking simple foods over a heat source, such as scrambled eggs or pancakes, either on an electric griddle or on the stove top.

BREAKFAST PREPARATION

Given proper access to the ingredients and tools necessary, a preschooler is also capable of serving themselves breakfast. Depending on their preferred breakfast choices, it is often possible to set out the ingredients they need ahead of time in a designated self-serve area and to just check periodically that everything is stocked and ready for the next morning.

For example, for a child who likes to eat a small bowl of cereal and milk in the mornings, you can keep two cereal options in sealed dry goods storage containers that have pouring spouts, along with a child-sized pitcher of milk on a lower shelf of the refrigerator. Since your child already has access to their own bowl and utensils, it is simple enough for them to select their cereal of choice in the morning, pour it into their own bowl, retrieve the milk pitcher and a spoon, and seat themselves at the table.

Another example might include keeping a small basket of fresh fruit available in a place that your child can easily access, along with a small container of granola and individual yogurt cups on a lower shelf of the refrigerator.

VISUAL RECIPES

A preschool-aged child can also easily follow visual recipe instructions for snacks, light meals, and simple baking recipes, which you can draw by hand ahead of time (no fancy artwork required, so long as it's clear), or you can simply take photos of each step and print them out for your child in the proper sequence. Alternatively, there are many visual recipe guides that have been created by parents and teachers, which can be readily purchased online to download and print. (See "Montessori Furniture & Materials: DIY Options.")

Visual recipe guides are a terrific way for your child to gain more practice in following a specific sequence of steps and become more independent in assembling snacks, small meals, and simple baked goods. Having readily available access to their own tools also greatly facilitates this process. However, the reality is that visual recipes won't always be available for every opportunity in the kitchen.

More often, your child will simply be working in cooperation with you as they assist in preparing larger family meals. And you just may be surprised and delighted to see how truly helpful your preschooler has become, given all of the tasks they are now capable of performing! It will genuinely begin to feel like a team effort, and your child will exude a sense of accomplishment in their work once the whole family sits down to enjoy the completed meal. It's not uncommon to hear a child exclaim proudly to a sibling or parent, "Did you know that I chopped these tomatoes all by myself?!"

With the proper guidance and tools, a preschooler can assist in the preparation and cooking of virtually any recipe. Even for what could be considered a more complicated meal, such as a layered lasagna, a preschool-aged child can easily perform most of the tasks.

From mixing the cheeses and seasonings in a bowl to preparing the meat sauce, filling a pot of water and placing the noodles into it for boiling, and actually assembling the lasagna layers one by one, a child is often eager and capable of assisting every step of the way. They find the smallest details fascinating and take great pride in accomplishing something that may feel difficult to them in the moment.

The key to success is in starting with enough time to move at a slower pace that your child can manage, as well as scaffolding the various tasks so that your child is able to help to the best of their ability. For example, your child might find it easy to pour the sauce onto the lasagna noodles in the pan but may need some assistance in successfully spreading the thicker cheese mixture on top. If your child encounters a task that they find particularly challenging, then simply invite them to continue trying for as long as they would like, and then step in to "take a turn" as you help to finish the job.

RECIPES FOR PRESCHOOLERS

EASY CHEESY MUFFINS

YIELD: 12 standard-sized muffins

2 cups self-rising flour
2 cups shredded cheese
2 cups milk

Optional add-ins: chives, diced ham, chopped bacon, mushrooms, baby spinach, bell peppers

Adult Prep: Preheat the oven to 350°F (175°C). Generously grease a muffin pan (or use paper cups). Gather all ingredients and tools, and place them on the table or countertop for your child.

1. Invite your child to measure out and pour all of the ingredients into the mixing bowl, and then use a child-sized wooden spoon to stir everything until thoroughly combined. (Note: you will need to assist as your child learns how to properly measure out ingredients, but they should be able to do it with increasing independence as their skill improves.)

2. Your child can then spoon the dough into the muffin cups.

3. *Adult Only:* Bake for 30 minutes, until lightly golden brown on the tops. Allow to cool for 15 minutes before removing to a wire rack to finish cooling.

TURKEY RANCH WRAP

YIELD: 1 full-sized wrap

1 tortilla wrap
2 slices of turkey deli meat
⅛ cup ranch dressing
1 large whole lettuce leaf (or ¼ cup chopped)
⅛ cup shredded cheese
⅛ cup diced tomato

Adult Prep: Gather all ingredients and tools, and place them on the table or countertop for your child.

1. Invite your child to measure out the ranch, shredded cheese, and diced tomato into small ramekins. (If you're planning to dice the tomato while making this recipe, then your child may also perform this step using a child-sized knife.)

2. Next, your child can place the tortilla wrap on a plate and use a child-sized spreading knife to spread the ranch dressing onto the wrap.

3. Your child can then add the turkey slices and lettuce and evenly sprinkle the shredded cheese and diced tomato over the top.

4. Finally, your child can roll up the tortilla and, if desired, cut it in half before serving.

BANANA BREAD

YIELD: 1 (4 x 8-in; 10 x 20cm) loaf

2 to 3 medium-sized overripe bananas

⅓ cup melted butter

1 tsp baking soda

Pinch of salt

½ cup sugar

1 tsp vanilla extract

1 large egg

1½ cups all-purpose flour

Adult Prep: Preheat the oven to 350°F (175°C). Generously grease a 4 x 8-inch (10 x 20cm) loaf pan. Melt the butter in the microwave (or on the stove top). Gather all ingredients and tools, and place them on the table or counter for your child.

1. Invite your child to peel and mash the ripe bananas with a child-sized masher in a mixing bowl until smooth. They can then carefully pour the melted butter into the mashed bananas and stir with a wooden spoon until combined.

2. Next, your child can measure out and add the baking soda, salt, sugar, and vanilla extract to the mixing bowl, and then stir again until everything is combined.

3. Your child can crack the egg into a small ramekin and lightly beat with a fork, and then add it to the mixing bowl, and stir again to combine everything.

4. Finally, your child can measure the flour and add it to the mixing bowl, stirring everything together one last time. Invite your child to pour the batter into the greased loaf pan.

5. *Adult Only:* Bake for 50 to 60 minutes or until a toothpick inserted into the center comes out clean. Allow to cool in the pan for a few minutes, then remove the loaf to a cutting board to cool completely.

BURRITO BOWL

YIELD: 4 servings

2 cups uncooked rice

1 lb (450g) lean ground beef

1 tbsp taco seasoning

1 (15oz; 425g) can black beans, drained

1 (2.25oz; 64g) can sliced black olives, drained

1 tomato, diced

1 avocado, diced

1 head romaine lettuce, chopped

Shredded Mexican cheese

Sour cream

Lime juice

Adult Prep: Gather all ingredients and tools, and place them on the table or countertop for your child.

1. Invite your child to assist in measuring and rinsing the rice, as well as helping with any steps involved in cooking the rice in a rice cooker or on the stove top (for example, placing the pot into the cooker or onto the stove, pressing button settings, etc.). Cook the rice according to package directions.

2. While the rice is cooking, your child can assist in chopping the tomato, avocado, and lettuce. Older children may also be able to operate a manual can opener to open the cans of black beans and sliced black olives.

3. *Adult Only:* Brown the beef, add the taco seasoning, and cook over low heat for 1 to 2 minutes more. Heat the beans separately in the microwave or on the stove top.

4. Invite your child to serve themselves a scoop each of the rice, ground beef, and black beans into their own child-sized bowl. Your child can also add their desired amounts of lettuce, tomato, avocado, and black olives, and then top with shredded cheese, sour cream, and a squirt of lime juice.

THE DINING AREA
EATING & MEALTIME

The social aspects of a family meal are highly valued in cultures all over the world, as adults and children sit down to eat together not only for the purposes of health and vitality but also as a means of connection and enjoyment.

Our children can only begin to understand the meaning of this special time together if they are provided the opportunity to both observe and fully participate as an included member of the family. However, in modern culture, it is common for an infant to be seated in a baby high chair for their meals, at different times and in a separate location from everyone else. The infant also has no independence in this arrangement, as they necessarily require the assistance of an adult to get into and out of the chair itself.

In the Montessori approach, the child's environment for mealtime looks much different. It takes into account the child's need for independence while also offering genuine respect for the child as another integral member of the family, no matter how young.

The child is provided with their own small table and chair, where they are easily able to seat themselves and from which they can begin taking their snacks and meals as soon as they begin eating solid foods. An adult is always present to sit with them, which reinforces the social value of sharing a meal together. From the very beginning, the child is also offered real metal utensils and a glass cup that are scaled down to a child's size so that they can successfully learn how to use them in the same way that they observe others in the family doing. They are also taught appropriate mealtime etiquette through modeling and kind, respectful reminders. And as the child grows older, they can begin to make use of a junior chair that allows them to join everyone else at the family table while still retaining freedom of movement.

In this chapter, we'll examine how to set up a simple, beautiful, and accessible environment for your child to use at mealtimes, as well as how to interact with your child in a respectful manner that fosters healthy attitudes about and appropriate behavior around food.

INFANTS

THE WEANING TABLE

As your infant first begins the gradual transition to eating solid foods, they should be seated at a child-sized table and chair, referred to as a *weaning table*. The height of the table and chair should both be low enough to the ground such that your infant can sit comfortably and their feet can touch the ground while seated.

At around six months of age, when your infant first begins using the weaning table, they will likely require your help to get into and out of the chair. However, as soon as they become mobile enough to crawl, they will quickly learn how to get in and out of the chair on their own, and the help of an adult will no longer be required.

On the weaning table should be a simple placemat containing clearly marked spots for the child's own plate, fork, spoon, knife, and cup. In the beginning, you can set the table for your child while they watch. Once your child is mobile and capable of retrieving these items on their own, you will discover that they find great joy in being able to set their own table.

Another element to consider including on your child's weaning table is a tiny vase of flowers or greenery, which will add an element of beauty to their dining space. Remember that even the youngest children appreciate these small details. And as your infant grows into toddlerhood, they will greatly enjoy being able to create their own small flower arrangements to place onto their weaning table.

It is essential that you remain at the weaning table with your child during mealtimes, especially in the beginning. Although you may not fit at the table itself, it's easy enough to sit on a small stool across from your child while they eat, perhaps even enjoying a small snack yourself at the same time. Not only does this allow you to safely supervise your child while they learn to eat solid foods, but it also reinforces the social aspects of sharing a meal together and allows your child to observe as you model proper mealtime etiquette.

When your child first learns to sit at the weaning table, it is easiest to place the back of their chair against a wall and scoot the table into the proper position. You can then gently prop your feet or knees against the table edge or legs to prevent the table from sliding forward if your child leans on it too much or if they try to push it away. This is only a temporary necessity, though, as your child will eventually gain enough stability to sit properly in their chair at the table.

INTRODUCING CUTLERY

In today's modern world of feeding babies, parents are bombarded with an endless array of specialized eating utensils, many of them touting "unbreakable" features and sleek, ergonomic designs. However, the Montessori approach emphasizes the use of *real* tools made of natural materials that are scaled down to a child's proportions—and this includes your infant's cutlery.

When selecting a fork, spoon, and knife for your baby to use at mealtimes, it's best to stick with an option that is most similar to what your child will see the rest of the family using. This will most likely be a set of very small, real metal utensils. (Although some families may prefer a set made of bamboo.)

Cutlery should be introduced to your infant in the very beginning of their solid foods journey—there is no need to wait. It's easiest to introduce the spoon first, followed shortly thereafter by the fork, once your child has gained experience in aiming properly for their mouth. A child-sized, blunt butter knife can be added once your child reaches toddlerhood and can make use of it.

When introducing each utensil, it's helpful to have two on hand—one for you and one for your baby. You can feed your baby with your spoon (if using this approach to feeding) while also allowing your baby to self-feed with theirs. This eliminates any possible battles over possession of the spoon. Alternatively, if you follow the baby-led weaning approach, then you will only need one spoon, to be used by your baby at their own choosing.

DRINKING FROM AN OPEN CUP

In keeping with the emphasis on the use of real tools, it is also recommended to offer your infant a real glass cup during mealtimes for drinking water. This guideline often takes new Montessori families by surprise because we are accustomed to the very common notion that glass isn't safe in the hands of a child (and especially not a baby!). However, there is a reason for the use of real glass, which we will discuss in a moment.

A glass cup should be introduced to your infant beginning with their first meal. The cup itself should be very small—about the size of a 2-ounce shot glass—and made of tempered glass so that it is less likely to break or chip if it is knocked onto the floor (which is likely to happen at least once). It is also helpful if the cup has ridges on the outside to assist your infant in keeping a firm grasp on the cup, although this may not always be possible depending on the brand.

When your infant first learns to drink from the cup, only fill it with a few sips of water. You will need to assist by allowing them to grasp the cup (if they want to) while helping to bring it to their lips. Don't pour the water into their mouth, as this will cause them to sputter; tip it back just enough to allow them to get a small taste. As your infant's skill improves over time, they will eventually be able to pick up, hold,

and drink from the cup, and then set it back down gently, all on their own. You can also fill it with increasingly greater amounts of water once you observe that your infant is becoming better at drinking. Once your child reaches toddlerhood, they can learn how to pour their own glass of water from a small pitcher throughout their meal as needed.

So why real glass? It helps your child to understand, through natural consequences, that they must exercise care when handling items in their environment. If the glass cup is ever accidentally broken, do your best to remain calm. Your first priority is to ensure your child's safety. Once this has been established, resist the urge to scold or punish. Instead, use it as a learning opportunity to help gently demonstrate for your child why they should be more careful when handling their glass cup. (However, if your child is in a throwing phase that makes safety an obvious concern, it may be prudent to temporarily offer a nonbreakable cup until the behavior subsides.)

EXPLORING FOOD

Food is the ultimate sensory experience for young children and especially for infants who are just learning to eat solid foods. The various colors, textures, smells, and tastes are all very intriguing and will naturally rouse a child's curiosity and desire to investigate.

When you first begin to introduce new foods to your infant, it's helpful to temper your expectations. Remind yourself that it's less about consuming a certain amount of food (at least before the age of 12 months) and more about exploration. Doing so will help to keep the experience positive and enjoyable for everyone.

Resist the urge to pressure your child into consuming a certain amount or different types of food during meals. Your role is simple: offer healthy options at mealtimes, and then allow your child to decide which foods and how much they want to eat.

You should also fully expect your child to use all of their senses to learn about the new foods being introduced to them, as their inner scientist goes to work trying to figure out everything they can about it. Lots of sniffing, spitting, squishing, and dropping (onto the floor) will be par for the course.

However, this isn't to say that mealtime should be a complete free-for-all without boundaries in the name of exploration. On the contrary, there are definitely a few simple and reasonable limits around mealtime, which, as long as they are consistently set, your infant will eventually learn to understand and respect.

As an example, it is reasonable to set the limit that your child should remain seated while eating. No food should be consumed while your child is up and about, not only for the

sake of proper etiquette but also for safety, as this could pose a choking risk. In addition, your child shouldn't be allowed to leave the table to crawl (or walk) around and play while they are actively eating. This limit should be set kindly but firmly from the very first time your child ever tries to leave the table during a meal (with or without food) and consistently again every time thereafter. You can offer a kind and gentle reminder of the expectation by saying something like, "You're leaving the table, which tells me that you're not hungry anymore. Let's take your plate to the kitchen." And then be sure to follow through on your statement. Your child will quickly learn that they must remain seated if they wish to continue eating. However, if they truly aren't hungry, then they should be allowed the freedom to leave the table and end the meal.

More common limits and how to set them will be addressed in the next section.

TODDLERS

THE JUNIOR CHAIR

Your child will likely continue to use their weaning table well into their toddler years. But depending on their size and mobility, they may also be able to start using a *junior chair* to join everyone else at the family table for some meals.

A junior chair is essentially a chair with an extra step built into the bottom of the legs so that your child has a place to rest their feet while they are seated. It's high enough that it can comfortably pull up to the height of a standard dining table, and some models are even adjustable such that the seat and footrest can be raised or lowered to accommodate a growing child.

Recall that freedom of movement is an important element of your child's independence. By offering your toddler a junior chair in lieu of a booster seat strapped to a regular chair, it becomes possible for your child to get into and out of it without needing an adult's assistance. And while some models do come with safety harnesses for the seat (enabling an adult to secure a much younger child into it), it is generally better to wait until your child is able to safely get in and out of a junior chair on their own before beginning to use it.

REFINING SKILLS

Toddlers are quite capable little beings when provided with the proper tools, modeling, and opportunity for practice. Over the course of just a few short months, your child will quickly master the use of the most common eating utensils.

The biggest hurdle to overcome in learning to use a spoon is remembering to orient the spoon in the proper direction so that food does not fall off, which may take some time. It can sometimes be difficult to sit on your hands and watch as your child experiments with how to accomplish this tricky maneuver, but take heart and have confidence that your child will eventually figure it out!

When it comes to your child's skill with a fork, having a real metal version to use will truly facilitate the learning process, since chunks of food are much more easily stabbed with metal fork tines than plastic ones. Food is also less likely to slide off metal tines when your child inevitably doesn't quite stab the chunk of food all the way, which will ultimately help to reduce their frustration.

A blunt, child-sized butter knife can also be introduced to your toddler. You can start out by simply offering one along with their other utensils during any meals in which they have an opportunity to observe others at the table using them. The odds are good that your toddler will be very interested in imitating what they see everyone else doing, and from there, it's only a matter of time and practice before they begin to get the hang of it.

In addition, your toddler can learn to use a small spreading knife to prepare a snack or small meal for themselves, such as spreading butter on a slice of bread; mashed avocado onto a piece of toast; and cream cheese, nut butter, or jam onto crackers.

Finally, depending on your family's food culture, you may also decide to introduce your toddler to eating with chopsticks. There are various versions of inexpensive training chopsticks that you can purchase, including some that are just attached at one end and require a squeezing motion (similar to tweezers), while others actually have finger loops to help your toddler learn to place their fingers properly.

SETTING THE TABLE

Toddlers love to be involved in a wide range of household tasks, especially those they have observed others in the home performing. One example of an everyday task that toddlers tend to find both challenging and enjoyable is learning to set their own table before a snack or meal. Although this can be introduced fairly early on, your toddler will likely begin showing more interest and ability around 15 to 18 months, once they are walking independently with ease and able to retrieve the various items that they will need on their own.

In order to help your child remember which items they need and where they should be placed on the table, you can provide a simple placemat that contains clearly marked outlines

for the plate (or bowl), spoon, fork, knife, and cup. Although there are many such placemats commercially available for purchase, you can also easily make one at home by drawing or sewing dark outlines onto any piece of sturdy, washable fabric (or any water-resistant material that easily wipes clean).

Be sure that your child's placemat, eating utensils, and dishes are stored somewhere that is low enough for them to access independently. When it is time to set the table, you can help to initiate your child's involvement by asking a question to get them started: "It's time for lunch; would you like to set your table? What do you need to get first?" Your child's specific process may not always be the most efficient, but do give them the time and space to do it in their own way, and try not to interfere (except when safety is a concern).

Aside from the items on your child's placemat, it may also be helpful to keep a child-sized pitcher of water or milk on the table for your child to fill their own glass at the start of the meal. Retrieving and filling this pitcher can become part of your child's regular routine when setting the table.

And as we discussed in a previous section, toddlers also appreciate an element of beauty in their dining area, just as an adult often enjoys eating at a table that includes soft candlelight or a vase of colorful, fresh flowers. Although it certainly isn't a required element for setting the table at every meal, you might find that your toddler takes great pleasure in periodically arranging a small vase of flowers that they can place on their own table to visually enjoy while they eat.

MEALTIME BEHAVIOR EXPECTATIONS

It is a natural part of every toddler's nature to test the boundaries that have been put into place. And although it may seem like it at times, do try to remember that they aren't doing these things on purpose to upset you. It's essential to reframe your perspective and recognize that your tiny toddler is merely allowing their inner scientist to take charge in that moment. As the parent, your role is to remain firm but also kind while setting limits on their less-than-desirable little experiments. Your goal is to gently guide them in *learning* which kinds of behavior are acceptable and which aren't.

How to respond when your child tries to leave the table during a meal was already addressed in the previous section on infants, as this is a common issue for parents whose children are first learning to sit at a table to eat. This may continue to be a limit you'll find yourself setting time and again for your toddler, and your response should always be the same.

But assuming your toddler has learned to stay at the table while eating, there are still plenty of other behavior expectations that you may find yourself needing to address at times. And as you'll see in the following common examples, your response is going to be quite similar each time, regardless of the individual behavior.

For example, if your child begins playing with or throwing their food (or dropping it onto the floor), then you can firmly and kindly say to your toddler: "You are playing with (or throwing or dumping) your food. That tells me you're not hungry anymore. Let's clean up and take your plate to the kitchen." You might choose to offer

this as a gentle reminder at first, to see if your toddler refocuses on eating, but if the behavior continues, then be sure to follow through.

If your child is using their utensils inappropriately, you might say: "You are banging your fork on the table. Your fork is for eating only. I'm going to put your fork away for now, and you can try again at dinner." And then allow them to finish the meal with their fingers.

And if your child is pouring their glass of water onto their plate or the table, the format of your response is still the same: "You are pouring your water onto your plate. Water must stay inside your cup for drinking. I'm going to put away your cup for now, and you can try again later." (Because your child needs to drink water, you can offer them a drink after a bit of time has elapsed, such as after the meal is over.)

Offering a consistent response each time sends your child the very clear message that these undesirable behaviors aren't acceptable. Your response is simply a logical consequence applied in a matter-of-fact way that shouldn't ever feel mean or punitive. And if your child becomes upset by the outcome of events, then you can still respond empathetically: "You're sad that the meal is over. It's hard to wait, but you'll be able to eat again at snack time."

Generally speaking, for most neurotypical toddlers without any nutritional or medical concerns, any kind of behavior other than eating during a meal is usually a pretty good indicator that they aren't very hungry anymore. And that's your cue to offer a gentle reminder of the expectation and follow through if the behavior continues.

PRESCHOOLERS

By the time your child has reached the preschool years, they have likely experimented on more occasions than you can count with lots of undesirable behaviors. But hopefully, they have also learned (thanks to your kind, firm, and consistent responses) that playing with food, throwing food on the floor, and walking around during a meal are not socially acceptable behaviors. That's not to say that your child will sit down and eat perfectly during every meal, but the chances are higher that their general behavior at the table is much less of an ongoing experiment at this age.

However, the preschool age also brings a shift in the focus of learning when it comes to mealtime. Your child is now more developmentally aware and capable of acquiring skills in grace and courtesy as they apply to various aspects of everyday life. *Grace and courtesy* is a term used to describe the polite behavior that we have come to expect in society, as well as in our own specific culture: for example, in greeting someone, saying "Thank you" and "Excuse me," pushing in a chair, or using a quiet voice indoors. Another important area is learning how to navigate the social graces of sharing a meal with others.

A great place to begin is by inviting your child to help with setting the family table before a meal. This task allows your child to feel like a valued, contributing member of the family and also fosters a sense of accomplishment, as there are so many small steps involved in properly setting the table for multiple people.

Set up your child for success by starting small, perhaps with inviting them to put out just the silverware. As their skill progresses, they can take on the responsibility of more steps in the sequence, including placing the plates, napkins, and cups, until they are capable of setting the entire table on their own. Be sure to store everything low enough that your child can access what they need, or set things out ahead of time for your child in a place they are able to reach. You can also make use of a transportable silverware caddy to help streamline the process a bit.

Your child's own process for setting the table may look a bit convoluted to you, and their final product may not turn out perfectly. You might even be tempted to offer suggestions that you know will make the job much easier. But remember that for a child, it's always about the process, not the end product.

Allow them the freedom to set the table in whatever order and manner they prefer, so as to preserve their focus and engagement with the task. If they get the sense that we are watching and judging, this could be enough to break their concentration and diminish their motivation.

Keep in mind that it's always an *invitation* to help. There may be times when your preschooler is simply not interested, and that's okay. It's not an assigned chore that we expect them to perform begrudgingly. There may also be times that your child will start but not finish the job completely, or they will place things in a way that must be fixed before the meal can be properly served and eaten. These situations, too, are okay. Just make a mental note to yourself to do it together the next time so that your child has an opportunity to observe the proper procedure. Then simply finish the job or adjust things as needed for that specific occasion.

Other aspects of grace and courtesy related to mealtime will likely be more specific to your family's own culture. Consistent modeling will be key in helping your child to understand which behaviors are socially acceptable.

For example, if you'd like for your child to say "please" and "thank you" or to politely ask someone to pass the bowl of carrots, then these are behaviors that you must demonstrate yourself.

And if there are other undesirable behaviors that your child exhibits, such as putting their feet on the table, try to avoid barking orders that focus on telling your child what *not to do*. ("Get your feet off the table!") Instead, offer them a gentle reminder of the expectation as you focus on communicating what you'd like for them *to do*: "Please put your feet back under the table. Thank you."

We can be fooled into thinking at times that our preschool child is old enough to "get it" and shouldn't be engaging in unacceptable behavior at the table. When this happens, remind yourself that they are still very young and most certainly *still learning*. Just focus on modeling the behavior that you *do* want to see, and try your best to remain patient, calm, and supportive whenever your child is showing you (with their behavior) that they need your gentle guidance.

THE PLAY SPACE
YOUR CHILD'S WORK

Children are both curious scientists and imaginative inventors. They enthusiastically explore any environment in which they find themselves with the keenest attention to detail and create their own play using whatever objects they happen to encounter.

Deep moments of play and learning are just as likely to happen in the sunny corner of a shared one-room apartment as they are in a family living room that doubles as a play area or in a dedicated playroom within a multilevel home. However, when designing a child's play space and curating a selection of toys and activities to include within it, there are certainly several aspects that should be given thoughtful consideration.

All too often, a child's play is dismissed as a more or less frivolous endeavor that serves no real, useful purpose. It's "just" play and therefore implied to possess a lesser value than the "real work" we engage in as adults. But as Dr. Montessori discovered through her observations of the children in her schools, a child's play *is* their work. A child regards their play with the same level of significance and gravity as would the CEO of any successful business. As new human

beings, they are in the process of developing themselves. They are eager to learn all that they can about how the world works and what their place is within it, and as such, every moment of play serves as an opportunity for the work of learning something new.

With this perspective in mind, it becomes easy to see why we should make an effort to take our child's play more seriously and to give careful thought toward the design of the play environment. Just as we might prefer an orderly, uncluttered, and aesthetically pleasing work space for ourselves in order to help us focus and feel more productive, our children are no different. Too many choices and lots of visual clutter will ultimately lead them to feel mentally overwhelmed, a lack of focus, and a loss of interest in the available toys and activities.

In this chapter, we'll take a closer look at the most important elements of designing the play space in your home such that it maximizes your child's ability to focus, concentrate, and engage in play that will help them develop to their fullest potential.

DESIGNING THE SPACE

When considering the overall design of the play area, your mantra should always be *less is more*. The primary goal is to create as little visual clutter as possible so that it's easy for your child to see which toys and activities are available and to be able to access them independently. The Montessori approach aligns fairly well with a minimalist perspective, in the sense that you'll be selecting fewer items to place on the shelf at one time. A good rule of thumb is to choose approximately eight to ten toys or activities per child, and even fewer if your child is still a very young infant. The remaining items can all be stored away and rotated periodically, which is a simple process that is covered in more detail later in this chapter.

ACCESSIBLE SHELVING

All of the toys or activities you select should be displayed on **low, open shelving** that is easily accessible to your child. A single-tier rectangular shelf, sometimes referred to as an "infant shelf," is ideal for babies who are not yet pulling themselves up to stand. In the earlier, more immobile months, an infant shelf is used to create a point of reference in their environment as the baby begins to observe the cycle of a parent selecting interesting toys and activities from the lowest part of the shelf, bringing them to the baby, and then putting them back on the shelf again after they lose interest.

As the infant grows and becomes more mobile through rolling, scooting, and crawling, their toys and activities are still placed within sight on the lowest part of the shelf so they can see and access all of their toys independently simply by moving over to the shelf. While an infant shelf can be one that is specifically built or purchased for this purpose in your child's play space, it is also possible to repurpose any floor-level shelf or small bookcase as an infant shelf. Once your child is pulling up to stand and eventually walking, slightly larger shelves with two or more levels can be used.

The selected activities can be displayed on the shelf for your child in an orderly and aesthetically pleasing manner by **using trays and baskets** to organize anything with multiple pieces. While there will likely be several toys that very obviously will not require a container (for example, a single wooden rattle or larger rolling bell cylinder), there will be many more activities that are clearly better presented on the shelf in a tray, basket, or some combination thereof. For example, a wooden frame puzzle can be presented to the child in a tray that contains a small basket of the puzzle pieces alongside the frame. A language basket containing small figurines and a set of cards for matching can be presented together in a single basket or tray. Use your intuition to choose a presentation style that makes the most sense to you.

It is also helpful to ensure that there is **generous spacing** of the available activities along the shelf. There should be very definitive "white space" between each item on the shelf so that things aren't stacked on top of or behind one another. Every basket or tray should have its own clearly designated spot on the shelf with an ample amount of empty space on either side of it. This translates to no more than three to four toys or activities per shelf level for a relatively standard 48- to 60-inch (122–152cm) length of open shelving. And if you're using a cube-style shelf, be sure to place only one item or activity within each cubicle. Trying to cram too many things onto a shelf at once creates the visual clutter that you are trying to avoid, in addition to making it less likely that your child will be able to retrieve and restore the activity to the shelf independently.

OTHER FURNISHINGS

Young children typically prefer to play directly on the floor, so comfort is something that should be taken into consideration. If the flooring in your child's play space is carpeted, then comfort will not likely be an issue. However, if there is only hard flooring present, then you might consider providing **a softer, padded area** for your child to play. For an infant, this can be a movement mat, which we will discuss in more detail later in this chapter. For a toddler or preschooler, you might potentially consider adding a small area rug.

At other times, older toddlers and preschoolers may also like to bring their work tray or basket to **a child-sized table and chairs**, depending on the amount of work space required for the activity they've selected. While these can sometimes be sourced secondhand in thrift stores, they can also be purchased brand-new at very budget-friendly prices from a variety of online retailers, as well as in most stores that carry children's furniture.

As for the display of books, we must recognize that it is very difficult for a young child to identify a book solely from its spine, especially before a child is able to read. Instead, it is ideal to always display books in such a way that the covers can be easily viewed by your child. This can be accomplished in a number of simple ways, such as standing up a small number of chosen books along a shelf or low windowsill, or by placing them front-facing into a sturdy basket for your child to flip through. Another option is to display them in a **front-facing bookshelf**, which allows all of the books to be displayed at once with the covers facing forward and at your child's eye level. This makes it easy for your child to readily identify and select their favorite titles independently. And if you're looking to save on floor space, you can install one or more picture-ledge style shelves that can easily hold several books in a forward-facing position.

AESTHETIC CONSIDERATIONS

Another aspect to take into account is the aesthetics of your child's play space. Dr. Montessori recognized that even very young children possess an innate appreciation for beauty in their environments, and so she emphasized that this element should not be overlooked. If painting the room where the play space is located, it's best to select a **clean, fresh, neutral color palette** for the walls. And if you decide to include an accent wall, try to choose a color or pattern that isn't too bright and visually overstimulating to your child. The inclusion of **high-quality artwork at the child's eye level** is an easy little extra that will also make the play space feel much more inviting and visually pleasing to your child. Skip posters and prints that look as if they specifically target young children, especially anything cutesy or commercial that includes cartoon characters or learning-oriented posters that might be found in a classroom setting. Instead, opt for beautiful photographs and paintings that represent the true work of an artist, not unlike something you might find in an actual museum.

One final aspect of the play space to consider is the intentional **inclusion of natural elements** within the environment. As much as an adult finds that the elements of nature tend to create a greater atmosphere of beauty and vitality, so do our children. As much as possible, bring nature indoors into your home and especially in the play space where your child is apt to spend a majority of their time. Select trays and bowls for activities made of natural wood, as well as cups and other practical life tools that are metal, glass, or ceramic. Try to choose toys made of these same materials over their plastic counterparts whenever possible. Open curtains to allow for natural sunlight to fill the room. Add some greenery to the space by including a real plant or two on top of a shelf or in a windowsill, and help your child learn how to care for it. You can also incorporate nature into the artwork that you select for the space by choosing beautiful photographs or realistic paintings of animals, plants, or landscapes.

SELECTING TOYS & ACTIVITIES

If you walk along the aisles of any toy store, you will quickly find yourself lost in a sea of plastic products that were specifically designed to attract and captivate our children's senses with bright colors, flashing lights, and music. Popular movie and TV characters are typically plastered all over the boxes in the hopes that our children will be drawn in by their favorites. Meanwhile, parents are primarily concerned with investing their hard-earned money in toys they believe will make their children happy.

But here's the rub: these kinds of toys are intended only to passively *entertain* our children and often do not require much creativity or imagination on their part beyond the push of a few buttons. And after a few moments, when the novelty has worn off, our children quickly lose interest and the toy is cast aside in favor of the next big thing. Ultimately, these kinds of toys are not much more than a false advertisement for the long hours of play that we perhaps envisioned when we initially decided to make the purchase.

So what kinds of toys and activities are actually worth the investment? To find the answer to this question, simply fall back on what you already know about the design of the play space itself: less is more! The *less* a toy actually does to passively entertain, the *more* opportunities there will be for your child to use

the toy in more novel and open-ended ways (hint: NOT the ones with flashing lights, buttons, and music).

An easy place to start is to adopt a new rule in your home: **avoid battery-operated toys**. Generally speaking, if it requires a battery, it's very likely that the toy is intended to do something to entertain your child. Instead, look for toys that require *your child* to do something with it in order to create play. A set of wooden blocks or a basket of play silks can literally become *anything* in the hands of a child. And the kind of play that happens with these more open-ended materials creates a much richer and stimulating experience for your child's growing imagination.

In addition to avoiding toys that require batteries, you can also specifically look for items that are made of **natural materials** instead of plastic. Wooden toys and materials tend to be higher in quality and have much greater longevity, as they are less likely to break over time. Natural materials also provide a better overall sensory experience; it's easy to recall from our own experiences how pleasing it feels to run your fingers over the smooth surface of an item made of wood or to sense its natural weight in your hand. Our children feel the same way! This guideline also applies to the materials used in practical life activities:

cups, pitchers, spoons, and other tools that are made of wood, metal, glass, and ceramic will always look and feel more inviting for our children to work with.

When selecting activities for your child's play space, you'll also want to consider the variety that you're providing at any one time. Typical "shelf work" in a Montessori environment often includes a variety of purposeful fine-motor tasks that aim to isolate one skill at a time. They also have a specific sequence of steps and target a desired outcome. Examples of these kinds of **close-ended activities** include completing a puzzle, sorting objects by color or size, transferring objects from one container to another using a variety of utensils, wet and dry pouring exercises, or matching objects to cards, just to name a few. Close-ended activities are greatly beneficial for our children because they tend to foster the development of focus and concentration, cater to their innate sense of

order, and make repetition possible so that mastery of a skill can be achieved.

However, Montessori play spaces at home are not limited to just these more purposeful kinds of shelf work. You should also provide a variety of **open-ended materials** for your child to use in their play, including such items as wooden blocks, train sets, magnetic tiles, Duplo/Lego bricks, play silks, bean bags, musical instruments, realistic-looking cars, dolls, and animal figurines, as well as items from nature. These kinds of materials are equally important to your child's development, as they allow for the necessary element of freedom during their play. There are no rules or limits as to what can be done with these materials and no pressure about making mistakes or doing something incorrectly. Children get to make their own rules and can experiment with as many scenarios and outcomes as they'd like.

Open-ended materials also help to provide fuel for your child's healthy imaginative play, as they will process events and situations from real life through role-play. They will use these materials to practice the real life skills that they're learning (for example, using a wooden block as pretend food for "cooking" or as a phone to "call" someone). They will likely also use their dolls and animals to play out their own versions of various social situations that they're actually experiencing in real life with siblings, friends, and other family members.

At certain times, you may find that your child isn't very interested in completing the activities you placed on the shelf and would much rather spend their time running and jumping about the house. This is especially common during the toddler years, when they are experiencing a very intense, developmentally appropriate need for movement. Your child's play space can easily cater to this need by offering opportunities to **support gross-motor movement.** If you have the available budget and space, you might consider adding one or two items to encourage large movement, such as a balance board, Pikler triangle, small climbing dome or wall, balance beam, indoor slide, set of "stepping stones," fabric swing, or foldable cushions. Otherwise, use the resources you have on hand! Allow your child more time to repetitively climb up and down the stairs (if you have them), or get creative with some pillows and chairs to set up a fun obstacle course. You can also take your child outside for

a walk off the beaten path; ride a balance bike or pedal trike; and encourage them to run, climb, and maneuver their way through nature's own obstacles.

ARTS AND CRAFTS MATERIALS

From the age of about 12 months old, you can also add a smaller, separate area somewhere in the play space for your child to work with arts and crafts materials. Placing a child-sized table and chairs in this area will not only provide your child with a designated spot to use these materials, but it will also help to set the limit from early on that art supplies should only be used in this area. This will greatly reduce the chances of your child engaging in "experimental" drawing on furniture and other household surfaces once they begin testing these boundaries. Store the materials near the designated table, either on a low shelf or in a small utility cart or chest of drawers, where your child can access them independently. Only leave out supplies that you have deemed safe for your child to use.

The specific types of arts and crafts materials you should make available will vary based on your child's age, fine-motor skills, and whether or not they are still in the habit of mouthing objects. It's usually a wise decision to select nontoxic and washable versions of art supplies whenever possible, as mistakes are bound to happen when these items are in the hands of young children.

When presenting arts and crafts materials to your child, always use supervision as well as your best judgment to help keep your child safe. Suggestions for age-appropriate materials might include:

- **12 to 18 months:** chunky or egg-shaped crayons, chunky colored pencils, construction paper, sidewalk chalk, nontoxic finger paint, play dough

- **18 months to 3 years:** chunky crayons and colored pencils, sidewalk chalk, dot markers, nontoxic finger paint, watercolor paint, solid tempera paint sticks, play dough, kinetic sand, stickers, safety scissors, construction paper, chenille stems, glue sticks, stamps

- **4 to 5 years:** regular crayons and colored pencils, regular chalk, markers, kinetic sand, stickers, blunt-tipped scissors, construction paper, chenille stems, liquid glue, stamps, ribbon, bits of fabric, pony beads, play dough, materials for collage, modeling or air-dry clay, watercolor paints, liquid tempera and acrylic paints, oil pastels

CHOOSING BOOKS

Even from the earliest days as a newborn, reading books with your child is a critical foundation of their language development. But not just any old book will suffice. It is essential to consider the quality of the books that are being read. The books you choose should help to ground your child in the reality of our world, as well as provide opportunities for exposure to rich vocabulary. There are several key features that you should look for in order to identify high-quality reading materials for your child's play space.

The most important aspect to consider is choosing books that are developmentally appropriate for your child. Infants, naturally having a very short attention span for reading,

will often prefer brief books containing simple pictures or photographs and only minimal words or phrases. As their fine-motor skills begin to develop during the first year, they will also begin to enjoy books with interactive components, such as touch-and-feel areas or flaps to open. Around the age of 12 months, you can expect your child's interest in and attention span for reading books with you to expand.

Toddlers love interactive books with touch-and-feel areas, flaps, and requests for simple actions using their face and/or body (e.g., "Now you touch your nose, too!"). They may also begin to enjoy books containing brief poetry, nursery rhymes, short stories, and nonfiction

material. (Usually anything that involves animals, vehicles, and the faces of other children will be a hit.)

Beginning in the preschool years, your child's love for reading (if it has been adequately nurtured thus far) will only continue to grow, especially as they begin showing interest in learning letter sounds and eventually reading on their own. Preschoolers will typically enjoy reading books that contain nursery rhymes, longer narratives, more advanced poetry, and nonfiction reference material on a range of scientific, geographical, historical, and cultural topics.

In keeping with the Montessori approach to fantasy versus reality for young children under the age of six, the books that you select should be realistic in plot, as well as in illustrations and/or photographs. Generally speaking, you will ideally try to avoid books that contain cartoon characters, pop culture references, anthropomorphized animals, creatures from fantasy, or plot lines that couldn't happen in real life.

You'll also want to aim for a balanced variety in the types of books that are available. Just because you're choosing realistic books doesn't mean that all of the books must necessarily be nonfiction learning and reference material. (Although these are indeed wonderful additions to your child's library, too). Your child's

bookshelf should also include lighter fiction books based in reality, containing plot lines that could actually happen in real life, as well as pictures or illustrations that look true to life.

As we also strive to raise children with a high degree of social and emotional intelligence, it can be especially helpful to include children's books on the topics of emotions, empathy, peace, and kindness in their collection. These areas, in particular, are often difficult for many parents to figure out how to navigate with their young toddlers and preschoolers. Having books about these subjects available in the play space can allow the time and space for some of those conversations to more organically occur.

Our children are the citizens of the future and so it is critical that we adequately prepare them for the global world they will ultimately inhabit. It is our responsibility to ensure that they have exposure to and experience with a wide range of cultures, abilities, and perspectives outside of our own families and local communities. An excellent way to set the stage for this learning is to include books that celebrate diversity and inclusion. Actively seek out books that embrace and positively portray main characters belonging to the global majority (e.g., Black, indigenous, and people of color), as well those with differing abilities and lifestyles.

SHELF ROTATION & TOY STORAGE

It's fairly likely that your child's toy collection is bigger than the recommended shelf limit of 8 to 10 toys, so what are you supposed to *do* with all of the other toys when they aren't out for use? The answer to this question is to establish a rotation system.

LET YOUR CHILD'S INTERESTS LEAD

Doing this is actually quite simple: using your child's current interests and skills to guide your selections, choose a limited number of toys or activities to place on the shelf, and temporarily store everything else somewhere out of your child's sight and reach. Your actual storage space will depend on the amount of toys your child owns. It could be as simple as a box that you store on a high shelf in a closet, or perhaps you need something larger and can dedicate some shelving space in a large closet or other area of your home for this purpose.

While some families feel that they need to have a set schedule to rotate their child's shelf (e.g., once a week or every month), it is actually better *not* to place this unnecessary pressure on yourself. Instead, approach shelf rotation from a true Montessori perspective: just follow your child's lead. Spend a few minutes each day observing your child while they play to see which toys or activities they seem to gravitate toward. These are the toys that you'll want to leave out on the shelf for now. Then mentally note which items look as if they have gone untouched for a while. (Maybe they're even collecting some dust!) It might be that these ignored toys are either too easy or too challenging for your child at the current moment, or perhaps your child is just more interested in other kinds of activities. (For instance, they'd rather be building block towers instead of completing a jigsaw puzzle.) Whatever the reason may be, these are the items that you should remove from the shelf the next time you're ready to rotate things. Place these ignored toys back into storage, and replace them with something else that is better aligned with your child's current interests.

SET EXPECTATIONS AROUND TOY STORAGE

You'll also need to figure out whether or not you want to rotate the shelf with your child present. Depending on their age and temperament, it may be possible to rotate things even while your child is playing right next to you. It's fairly easy to do this with infants and young toddlers, as they aren't quite as cognizant of exactly what it is that you're doing. However, as your child gets closer to the preschool years, they will be much more aware of and interested in what you're doing with their toys and where you're storing them. At this point, it may be easier to wait until a time when your child is not present. This might be during your child's nap or after bedtime, when they're at childcare or school, or while they are in the care of another adult.

Finally, what do you do if your child asks you for a specific toy that is in storage? When this happens, you have two options: The first is to kindly and gently let your child know that the item is currently in storage but that you will make sure to put it back on the shelf during the next rotation. (And then don't forget to keep your word.) The second option is to simply retrieve the item for your child, especially if this request isn't common practice for your child and you feel okay about retrieving it. Just know that it's possible your child might inadvertently learn that you'll take things out of storage for them any time they ask, and this may not be an expectation you want to set yourself up for. So decide ahead of time what your plan of action will be and follow through with it as consistently as possible.

A note about book rotation: Just as you rotate the toys on your child's shelf, you should also periodically rotate their books. Again, try to follow your child's lead by periodically swapping out ignored books for different ones that better align with your child's changing interests and skills, as well as the seasons, holidays, and any other topics that your child is learning about at home. Be sure to always keep a few of their tried-and-true favorites on the shelf, too. Incorporating regular library trips into your family's weekly rhythm can also be a great way to try new books without having to spend the money to buy them up front.

HOW TO ORGANIZE A SHELF

If there were one aspect of your child's playroom that you would want to dedicate a few extra minutes of careful thought toward, it's the actual organization of the shelf itself. Your goal is not only to curate a beautifully inviting shelf of toys and activities that will entice your child into deeper play but to also craft a space that is functional for your child's learning. And there is elegance in a minimalist approach.

USE A SHELF MAP

The best way to achieve a curated learning space is to create a shelf "map" for yourself. Grab a piece of paper and make a rough sketch of your child's shelf. Along each shelf, draw approximately three to four defined spaces that will house *just one* toy or activity at a time. Remember to leave plenty of empty space on the shelf between activities so that everything clearly has its own spot and things don't appear too cluttered. For a single-tier infant shelf, these three to four activities may be the only ones that you have available at any given time. For a two-tier toddler or preschool shelf, your total count is likely to be somewhere in the ballpark of 8 to 10 activities (depending on the length of your shelf and the actual sizes of the toys or activity trays that you're placing on it).

WORK WITH CATEGORIES

In each dedicated activity space that you've drawn on your shelf map, write down a single category of toys or activities that you might want to place there. For infants and toddlers, it's easiest to choose categories that are loosely skills-based. Just a few possible examples might include objects for grasping, sorting by size, opening and closing activities, musical instruments, learning colors, exercising the pincer grasp (e.g., peg puzzles), or language work. However, the actual categories that you decide upon will depend entirely on your child's current stage of development. And this being the case, you will also see that the categories you initially choose will continue to evolve as your child grows.

For young preschoolers, you can certainly still use a skills-based system of organization. However, as your child's skills become more refined, it will become clear that they are ready for more challenges. They may also begin to display a greater interest in academic learning. Once this occurs, it is better to shift your organization system toward one that correlates more to the various Montessori subject areas of language, mathematics, sensorial development, practical life, and cultural studies (which includes science, history, and geography). You might also choose to designate a shelf space for music and/or art activities, unless you've already created a separate space for these activities. This will ensure that you are delivering a wide range of activities for play and learning instead of putting too many of the same kinds of activities on the shelf at once or repeatedly.

Using categories like these to help organize your child's shelf can also be of great assistance as you observe your child during their play because it will easily allow you to see at a glance which skills and/or learning areas your child is actively gravitating toward and which ones they may not be expressing an interest in. Then it becomes much clearer which kinds of toys or activities, based on your shelf map, might need to be rotated out in lieu of something easier or more challenging. You might also need to replace an item with something new altogether if it has been out for a while and your child has finally lost interest in it. Then it's just a matter of taking a quick trip to your storage area to swap the item out for something different.

Do keep in mind that the use of categories is only intended to act as a guide in your organization system. It is not set in stone and should be adjusted in any way that you see fit, according to the needs and interests that your child is expressing. For example, if your three-year-old is beginning to show more interest in learning about letter shapes and sounds but does not appear at all interested in mathematics, you might decide to have more than one shelf space dedicated to language work and none that include mathematics for the time being. There is no reason to limit your child's choices based solely on a theoretical idea of what "should" be on the shelf. Your child is always growing and changing, and so their play space should change accordingly. If you always defer to your observations of your child for guidance in making such decisions, it's really difficult to go wrong.

HOW TO ARRANGE A WORK TRAY

Before you are finished physically organizing your child's toys and activities on the shelf, it is also necessary to consider one final aspect: the visual presentation of the activity itself. A clear, purposeful selection and arrangement of an activity's pieces on a tray can quite literally make or break your child's decision to engage with the material.

Not every activity will require a tray. Some activities will make more sense when placed in a basket (for example, a selection of animal figurines and their associated matching cards). Still other activities might be too large for a basket or tray or just might be better presented alone on the shelf (for example, a large spinning drum). It's really going to require your own personal judgment to make a determination on a case-by-case basis.

For any activities that you've determined will require a tray (of which there will likely be many), your efforts in giving some forethought to how it *looks* on the tray will pay off later when your child is visually drawn to the activity on the shelf and is able to independently use the materials in a logical manner.

Here are a few rules of thumb to keep in mind:

- **Present activities "undone":** Avoid placing things on the shelf that are already done for your child. For example, instead of placing a completed puzzle frame on the shelf, try putting all of the pieces into a small basket, and place it next to the empty puzzle frame in a tray. Another example might include placing the rings from a wooden stacker toy into a basket and placing it next to the empty vertical peg base. Something that looks like it needs to be put back together again in some way is always much more enticing to a curious child!

- **Arrange items from left to right:** To reinforce foundational reading skills, always try to organize the items on a tray in the same fashion as your child will eventually learn to read (in English), which is beginning on the left and moving toward the right. So in the previous puzzle example, the basket of puzzle pieces would be placed *to the left* of the empty puzzle frame on the tray. By doing this, your child will naturally begin by taking a puzzle piece from the left and moving toward the right to place it into the frame. Or if you're presenting a dry-pouring activity that includes two small pitchers, then you'll place the pitcher that contains all the dried rice or beans on the left so that this automatically becomes the natural place for your child to start as they pour all of the beans into the pitcher on the right. This rule is especially important for any activities that contain a sequence of multiple steps; try to arrange the various materials on the tray such that your child will naturally and logically pick them up to use them in sequence from left to right as they work through the activity. Depending on the activity, this won't *always* be possible, but it's worth experimenting with a few different layouts on the tray to find one that most closely approximates a left-to-right orientation.

- **Consider aesthetics:** Young children possess a deep appreciation for and attraction to elements of visual beauty, so put on your inner interior designer hat for just a few moments to consider the specific colors and materials that you're using together on the tray. Your goal is to make the tray look as inviting as possible so that your child *wants* to handle the materials and engage with the activity upon seeing it. Is there a way that you can color coordinate any of the elements to help tie it all together? For example, you might purposely choose to use a small orange bowl or clean-up sponge to complement an orange juicing activity. Or if an activity already has a lot of wooden elements, then you might consider adding a small pop of color or beauty somewhere else on the tray by intentionally choosing to use an ornate metal spoon or a pretty ceramic bowl to help it stand out, which will naturally draw your child's eye and attention to that part of the activity.

HOW TO PRESENT AN ACTIVITY

Some of a child's toys, especially those of a more open-ended nature (e.g., wooden blocks), will not require an adult to demonstrate their use. Children just seem to already *know* what needs to be done with these things and so their innate creativity will naturally lead them to experimentation with the many possibilities.

However, there will be some shelf work that will require an initial presentation from you so that your child understands how the materials are intended to be used. Typically, these will be the activities that are more purposeful and close-ended. Some examples include the demonstration of fitting jigsaw puzzle pieces together for the very first time, how to carefully pour water from a pitcher to a glass, or properly threading a shoestring through the holes of a lacing card.

SHOW, DON'T TELL

As a highly verbal species, we prefer to use language in communicating our thoughts to others, which is perfectly acceptable when we are conversing with other adults. However, young children, who are only just beginning to acquire language, are not as easily able to learn from auditory instruction alone. When we speak, our children tend to be highly focused on our mouths; they closely watch our lips to see the formation of our words to better understand what we are saying.

When we present a new activity to our child, what we want is for them to *watch* what we are doing with our hands. They simply cannot do this if they are distracted by watching our mouths while we speak. Thus, it is a better approach to limit talking and instead focus on showing your child what to do.

We also need to consciously slow down our movements. Adults generally move way too quickly for a child to process what's happening, and then we end up having to repeat our actions to help them understand. Instead, we must remember to intentionally use slow, careful motions with our hands so that our child actually has an opportunity to take in all of the details.

AN EXAMPLE IN ACTION

What does this look like in practice? Take, for example, the most basic presentation of pouring water from a small pitcher to a glass. In our typical, overly wordy adult manner, while also moving far too quickly, we might say to a toddler, "See the handle here? Just pick it up like this . . . and then carefully tip it over and pour it into the glass . . . like this. Try not to spill any when you're pouring! Now stop when the water gets this high so it doesn't overflow. And then put the pitcher back down. See how I did that? Okay, now you try!"

But all your child is going to absorb from this kind of demonstration is: "Pour the water into the glass." Although we obviously would never expect perfection from our toddler's very first attempts with this activity (it's going to be messy no matter what!), they are already at a greater disadvantage in experiencing success because they weren't given an opportunity to really absorb the finer details of careful pouring.

Instead, try presenting the activity with far fewer words (or even none at all) as your child intently watches the slow, careful movements of your hands and fingers. Pause for a moment in places where you want your child to notice something important. It might surprise you to learn that children are actually able to suss out many of the finer details on their own without any verbal instruction required.

This might look something like this: "I'm going to show you how to pour the water into the glass. Watch." Moving slowly, point to the handle of the pitcher, and pause for a moment. Grasp the handle gently with your fingers, then slowly move your other hand in to support the pitcher just under the lip. Pause again. Slowly and carefully lift the pitcher, then move it over to the open glass. Pause for a moment, and then begin to slowly pour the water into the glass. (In these first presentations, you should only provide enough water in the pitcher to naturally fill the glass without overspilling.) Once nearly all the water has been poured out, pause, and then gently tip the pitcher to look inside, checking to see if any water is left. Slowly pour the last drop of water into the glass, and then gently set the pitcher back down on the tray.

It's also helpful to "make mistakes" as your child is likely to do so they can observe how to handle the situation properly. For example, you might spill a drop or two and use the sponge to clean it up. Finally, repeat these same slow, careful movements to pour the water from the glass back into the pitcher, effectively resetting the activity for your child. Then, turn to your child and say, "Now it's your turn."

THE INFANT'S MOVEMENT AREA

For the majority of the first year, infants are fairly immobile. Up to about three to four months of age, a newborn will require direct assistance from an adult in the exploration of their environment. They will need to be carried to certain areas if they need a change of scenery, and toys must be brought to them for interaction, as they cannot yet do this for themselves. Once a baby begins reaching for and grasping objects on their own, sitting up, and eventually scooting themselves about on the floor, a whole new world of possibilities opens up for them in terms of independent exploration.

Beginning from birth, your newborn baby can be placed in a Montessori movement area for quiet observation and play time. If possible, this space should not be isolated to your child's bedroom, where they would otherwise be separated from everyone else during play time. Ideally, the movement area should be located in closer proximity to a communal space in your home—such as the living room—or incorporated as part of an already-established play space for older siblings, where your baby can observe and listen to the ebb and flow of life's daily activities even as they play.

When setting up your infant's movement area, consider including a low infant shelf that houses just three to four toys or activities, as well as a cozy mat or rug to lay on as they play. Your baby's ability to view their environment from the floor is fairly limited while they are still very small and immobile, so you can also add a floor-level mirror (either safely mounted on a nearby wall or purchased as a freestanding unit). This will offer your infant a better view of what's going on in the room from any position they might find themselves in. A mirror also enables your baby to see themselves, which is a favorite pastime of most infants. And for newborns, you might also consider suspending a Montessori mobile safely out of reach—about 12 inches (30.5cm)—above your baby's head/chest in the mat or rug area to help develop your baby's visual and tactile senses. A mobile can easily be suspended from the ceiling using a plant hook and metal key ring or, alternatively, from a wooden activity gym.

THE MONTESSORI MOBILES FOR INFANTS

There are a series of four traditional **Montessori visual mobiles** that can be used with newborns, which are designed to be presented chronologically as your baby grows. In proper order, they are:

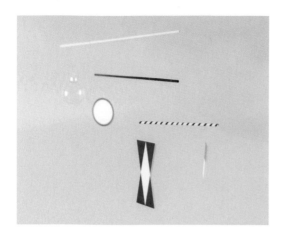

Munari mobile (3–6 weeks old): Presented to the newborn is a series of high-contrast geometric shapes that follow a precise formula based on the size of a glass sphere. All of the shapes are perfectly counterbalanced such that the slightest wisp of air will set them moving in a slow, rhythmic manner that develops the infant's ability to focus on and visually track an object.

Octahedron mobile (5–8 weeks old): At just the right time for the beginning development of an infant's color vision, this mobile presents three octahedron shapes in red, blue, and yellow. The reflective quality of the octahedrons helps to foster the infant's ability to focus and concentrate and lays a foundation for an understanding of future geometrical concepts.

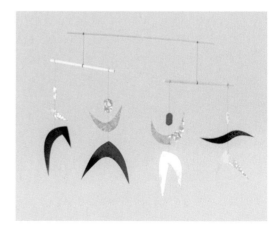

Gobbi mobile (7–10 weeks old): At this age, an infant is beginning to perceive subtle variations in color. A set of five small spheres in graded shades of the same color are suspended at a 45-degree angle from a single rod with the darkest shade at the lowest position and the lightest shade at the highest position.

Dancers mobile (8–12 weeks old): Toward the end of the first three months, an infant's color vision is nearly fully developed. This mobile, composed of several human figures made of reflective paper, focuses on helping to develop depth perception and the ability to track moving objects.

As soon as your infant is trying to reach for, bat, grasp, and mouth objects (typically around three to four months of age), you can start introducing **Montessori tactile mobiles** in the movement area, which are intended to help develop hand-eye coordination and allow your baby to exert some control over their own environment. The mobile should be suspended from a length of ribbon or elastic cord just above your baby's hands and chest area and at a height they can easily reach.

There isn't a specific order for when to introduce the tactile mobiles, so spend some time observing your baby to see which motor skills they're working on and choose a mobile that best suits those needs. To help you get started, here are a few ideas:

- **Bell on a ribbon:** A single small bell is attached to the end of a long ribbon. As the infant begins to hit the bell, they learn there is a connection between the motions of their arms/hands and the sound of the bell. This mobile is usually the first tactile mobile to be introduced.

- **Ring on a ribbon (or elastic cord):** A single wooden or metal ring is attached to the end of a long ribbon. The infant is able to reach for and grasp the ring. If using an elastic cord, the infant is able to bring the ring to their mouth.

- **Bell chimes mobile:** A circle of four natural wooden bells surrounds a large wooden bead on a string in the middle, which is also connected to a hanging wooden ring. The infant is able to bat at or grasp the ring in order to move the bells to make them gently rattle. If this mobile is securely suspended from an elastic cord, then the infant can also pull the ring to their mouth.

- **Montessori puzzle ball:** A stuffed fabric ball with a fascinating design, having several little nooks for an infant to grasp and explore. It may also have a small bell inside or attached to one end. The ball can be suspended above your baby's chest for grabbing or a bit closer to your baby's feet for kicking.

Ready-made versions of most Montessori mobiles, both visual and tactile, can easily be purchased online. However, if you're the crafty type and enjoy a good DIY project, then there are also plenty of ways to make them yourself with simple craft supplies or by using toys and materials you already have on hand. A quick Google search will typically yield dozens of tutorials that you can easily follow.

There also aren't any limits on how long to leave a mobile in your infant's movement area. Each one can be presented for as long as your baby remains interested in it. Once you begin to notice that a particular mobile is no longer capturing your baby's attention, then consider replacing it with the next visual mobile in the series or a new tactile mobile that is better suited to their developing motor skills.

INFANT ACTIVITIES

The following list comprises a sampling of both traditional Montessori and Montessori-inspired activities that are appropriate for babies up to 12 months old. Although general age suggestions are provided for each activity, they are intended only as general guidelines. All children develop on their own timeline, and your baby may be ready sooner for some activities while needing a bit longer for other activities. Just relax, have fun, and enjoy your baby!

NEWBORN RATTLE (0–3 MONTHS)
This rattle consists of a small wooden dowel with a bell secured to each end, enabling your newborn to exercise the grasping reflex. The soft sound of bells jingling as your baby moves their arm will catch their attention, making for a great first experience with cause and effect.

GRASPING BEADS (4+ MONTHS)
A set of several chunky wooden beads securely strung together on a hemp cord will help to strengthen and refine your infant's grasping skills. They also offer relief from teething pain.

HIGH-CONTRAST CARDS (0–3 MONTHS)

A set of cards featuring simple black-and-white patterns can be placed on the wall near your infant's changing or movement area to engage their visual sense. Allow your baby to focus on the images for as long as they'd like. To promote continued engagement, rotate image positions or change out the images periodically.

SMALL BELL CYLINDER (4+ MONTHS)

Infants enjoy grasping, mouthing, and shaking this toy, which is simply a small wooden cylinder with a small bell inside. It's great for sensory development and exploration of cause and effect.

SENSORY BALLS (4+ MONTHS)

Balls will always be a fan favorite among infants and toddlers, and your baby is finally ready to begin the fun! Offer a variety of balls with interesting patterns, colors, sizes, and textures to help stimulate your infant's visual and tactile senses. Start a collection of balls as you discover new ones over time.

SPINNING DRUM (4+ MONTHS)

This colorful wooden drum smoothly rotates around a horizontal dowel and usually contains a loose marble inside. As your infant spins the drum with their hand, both the visual and auditory senses are engaged. This activity also fosters purposeful hand and wrist movements and encourages reaching for objects. It can be placed in front of your baby during tummy time or while sitting independently.

MUSICAL INSTRUMENTS (4+ MONTHS)
A young infant can be offered simple musical instruments to grasp, shake, and explore, such as an egg shaker, maraca, bells, or a small tambourine. As your baby grows older and you begin to see signs of more intentional exploration of cause and effect, you can provide new instruments to try!

SCARF BOX (6+ MONTHS)
This activity is an easy DIY to make at home: just save an old, reusable baby wipes container (or tissue box), and fill it with light silk scarves or baby washcloths. Allow your infant to pull all of the scarves out of it, then refill it for baby, and repeat!

INTERLOCKING DISCS (6+ MONTHS)
A set of two round, wooden discs that interlock with one another: a shape that is perfect for developing an infant's hand-to-hand transfer skills. They also wobble when slowly rolled across the floor, providing a point of interest and motivation for your baby to practice crawling after it.

WOODEN RING STACKER (6+ MONTHS)
The wooden rings in this activity are all wide and equally sized, making it an ideal first opportunity for the development of your infant's hand-eye coordination.

SENSORY FABRICS (6+ MONTHS)

Offer your infant a variety of small fabric pieces in a basket to freely explore through sight and touch. This activity is easy to DIY if you have spare fabric or old clothing that can be repurposed.

SENSORY SHAKERS (6+ MONTHS)

This is another simple DIY activity that provides an interesting sensorial experience for an infant. Fill 4 to 5 empty spice jars with various household pantry items, such as rice, beans, dried spices, salt, etc. Glue the lids shut (for safety), and allow your baby to explore them by looking, shaking, and listening.

THEMED TREASURE BASKET (6+ MONTHS)

In this activity, an infant is offered a basket filled with 5 to 7 items that all belong to the same category: kitchen utensils, farm animal figurines, vehicles, items from nature, etc. Your baby should be encouraged to explore the basket freely and independently. (Although you can also name the items at other times to help promote vocabulary development.)

CIRCLE-SHAPE KNOBBED PUZZLE (9+ MONTHS)

Your infant will practice hand-eye coordination and unknowingly absorb an early understanding of basic geometric shapes as they learn how to place a single-shape puzzle piece correctly into its puzzle frame. Offer a circle shape first, as this is the easiest shape to master. Once your baby's skills improve, begin to offer other shapes.

BALL CYLINDER (9+ MONTHS)
A favorite game of infants in this stage is to repeatedly push items across a floor and crawl after them. A ball cylinder provides the perfect motivation for this activity, as it will easily roll away while making an attractive sound.

OBJECT PERMANENCE BOX (9+ MONTHS)
This classic Montessori activity helps an infant develop their understanding of the concept of object permanence—that if something (or someone) disappears from view, it isn't gone forever. As your baby places a ball in the hole at the top of a box, it disappears momentarily but reappears a moment later as it rolls back out into the tray.

EGG IN CUP AND PEG IN CUP (9+ MONTHS)
These 3D puzzles are another classic Montessori infant activity. The infant first learns to place the egg into its cup, and once this has been mastered, they move on to the more difficult task of placing the peg into its cup. Both are great for hand-eye coordination, focus, and concentration.

IN-AND-OUT WORK (9+ MONTHS)
Infants love to repeatedly place objects into containers and take them out again. Offer choices to help your baby explore this urge: any small container, such as a pail, bucket, jar, box, or basket—and something to drop into it, like a ball, wooden peg, or block. A Montessori "box with bins" is a great tool for this activity, as you can hide little items inside the drawers for your baby to discover!

INFANT COIN BOX (9+ MONTHS)

Several wooden coins are placed into a slot on the top of a box and a sliding drawer underneath must be opened in order to retrieve them. You can DIY this activity by repurposing any lidded food container (e.g., an oatmeal canister). Cut a thin, rectangular hole in the lid for your baby to drop in several old gift cards (or a circular hole for several extra-large pom-poms).

LANGUAGE BASKET (9+ MONTHS)

An infant's development of new vocabulary can never begin too early! Place 3 to 4 objects of the same category into a basket for your baby to explore (e.g., fresh fruit, animal figurines, kitchen utensils). Pick up each object one at a time, and show your baby while naming each out loud: "This is an orange." Allow them to explore the basket of objects for as long as they desire.

CARDS IN A WALLET (9+ MONTHS)

This activity encourages the use of the pincer grasp. Save several used gift cards and place them inside of an old wallet. Allow your baby to investigate the wallet and remove the cards. Once some or all of the cards have been removed, you can place them back into the wallet (if your baby isn't yet attempting to do so on their own), and offer an opportunity to repeat the activity.

PINCER GRASP BLOCK (9+ MONTHS)

In this activity, an infant refines the use of the pincer grasp by removing a small, knobbed wooden peg from its block using the thumb and forefinger, and then replacing it again. Allow your baby to repeat the activity for as long as they remain interested.

WALKER WAGON (12+ MONTHS)

A walker wagon is an immensely helpful tool for your baby to discover their ability to walk independently without the help of an adult holding their hands. They can push it along as they practice their balance, and as a soon-to-be toddler, they will eventually also begin using it to transport toys and other objects around your home.

PULL TOY (12+ MONTHS)

An infant who is already walking may also greatly enjoy having a pull toy to pull behind them as they practice independent walking, which helps to refine gross-motor movements and coordination of balance. Babies who aren't walking yet may also enjoy using the string to pull the toy toward themselves from a seated position.

TODDLER ACTIVITIES

The following is a sampling of both traditional Montessori and Montessori-inspired activities that are appropriate for toddlers from one to two years old. Although general age suggestions are provided for each activity, they are intended only as a general guideline. All children develop on their own timeline, and your toddler may be ready sooner for some activities while needing a bit longer for other activities. Remember to relax and follow your child!

FITTING LIDS TO CONTAINERS (13+ MONTHS)
Develop your child's fine-motor skills and build concentration by offering a tray containing several different small containers with different types of lids (jars, Tupperware, empty food canisters, etc.). Your toddler can practice taking the lids on and off of the containers.

COLORED RING STACKER (13+ MONTHS)
This popular children's toy allows toddlers to practice hand-eye coordination by learning how to place the colored rings accurately onto the vertical dowel. Your toddler will not be able to correctly place them in size order yet, though, as that skill develops sometime around two years of age.

MULTIPLE SHAPE KNOBBED PUZZLE (13+ MONTHS)

Toddlers are ready for more complex puzzles than the single-shape knobbed variety. Offer your child a knobbed puzzle frame containing a few simple shapes, such as a square, circle, and triangle.

IMBUCARE BOX (13+ MONTHS)

This classic Montessori activity hones your child's hand-eye coordination. Begin with a circle, as this is the easiest, and progress to offering more complicated shapes with more sides as your toddler masters each one. A DIY version of this activity can be created using any cardboard box with a lid, along with blocks of various shapes. (Or make the shapes out of cardboard.)

NESTING BOXES, CUPS, AND BOWLS (13+ MONTHS)

Offer your child a set of nesting boxes or cups (or just use a set of measuring cups or mixing bowls from your kitchen) to practice ordering objects by size. You don't have to offer all of the pieces at this point, as too many can be confusing for a young toddler. Stick to offering just 3 or 4 objects at a time until your child's skills progress.

OPEN-AND-CLOSE WORK (13+ MONTHS)

Offer a basket containing a variety of small bags, purses, and boxes with different types of closures. You can also offer an assortment of small jars and containers with different kinds of lids. Begin by offering simple, easy-to-open closures, and progress to more difficult ones over time. Once your toddler stops putting things into their mouth, you can also put small trinkets inside the containers for your child to discover.

DISCS ON A HORIZONTAL DOWEL (13+ MONTHS)
As toddlers master the vertical dowel ring stacker, they are usually ready to try performing the same activity using a horizontal dowel. This activity is more difficult, as it requires your child to cross the midline of their body in order to slide the discs onto the dowel.

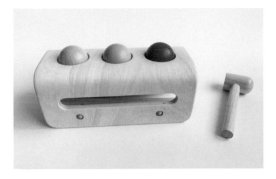

BALL POUNDING BENCH (13+ MONTHS)
Toddlers can practice their hand-eye coordination and gross motor skills by pushing the balls into the holes, which is always great fun. Your child may only use their hand to push the balls through at first but will eventually progress to pounding them using the wooden hammer.

SHAKER AND TOOTHPICKS (13+ MONTHS)
Offer your toddler a spice jar with large holes and several blunt toothpicks. Demonstrate how to place the toothpicks into the holes, then how to shake them out (or remove the lid), and repeat. Another variation is to cut holes in the lid of an old food container (e.g., an oatmeal canister) in which to place wooden popsicle sticks. As your toddler grows, you can color coordinate the holes and sticks for color matching.

GROSS-MOTOR MOVEMENT (13+ MONTHS)
Toddlers seem to be in constant motion, and they love to experiment with all the different ways that they can move their bodies. Provide opportunities for your child to run and climb as much as necessary by offering a rocking horse, junior slide, Pikler triangle, flight of stairs, homemade obstacle course with pillows, or time at the playground, as well as practice with throwing, catching, and kicking a large ball.

LOCKS AND LATCHES (16+ MONTHS)

Locks and latches are not only very intriguing for toddlers, but they also help to hone fine-motor skills. Although your child may only be able to open some of the locks and latches at this point (and may or may not yet be able to close them back up again on their own), with continued practice over time, they will eventually come to master all of them.

SMALL-KNOBBED PEG PUZZLES (16+ MONTHS)

As your toddler's fine-motor skills and hand-eye coordination are quickly growing, you can offer a new level of challenge with peg puzzle frames that have smaller-knobbed pieces to help them exercise their pincer grasp.

OBJECT-TO-OBJECT MATCHING (16+ MONTHS)

Offer your child a basket of 3 to 4 matching sets of different objects in one category. For example, a basket of kitchen utensils might include two identical forks, two metal pitchers, and two wooden spoons. You can also use matching animal figurines, vehicles, fresh fruit, and items from nature (pine cones, rocks, leaves, etc.). Encourage your child to find and pair the matching items together.

SHAPE SORTER (16+ MONTHS)

A child who has had some experience with imbucare boxes is ready for a shape sorter containing several different shapes to sort at a single time. This activity helps to further refine their understanding of early math concepts and hand-eye coordination.

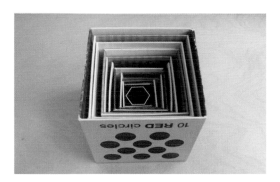

STACKING BOXES (16+ MONTHS)
Toddlers love the challenge of learning to balance and stack boxes by size atop one another. This activity is great for hand-eye coordination, practicing visual discrimination by size, and gross-motor work. A DIY version of this activity can be created by repurposing a variety of empty boxes (from cereal boxes, packages, etc.) that have been taped shut.

MATRYOSHKA NESTING DOLLS (18+ MONTHS)
This activity promotes a toddler's fine-motor skills, hand-eye coordination, and cognitive development. As they discover how to take apart the nesting dolls, they will also begin to experiment with how they fit back together and nest inside one another.

LACING BEADS (18+ MONTHS)
As a toddler learns to carefully place the tip of a shoelace through chunky wooden beads in order to string them together, they are building their hand-eye coordination, concentration, and fine-motor skills. This activity also lays the foundation for later sewing work.

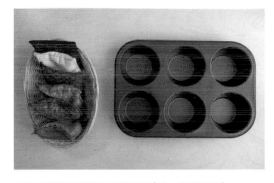

1-TO-1 CORRESPONDENCE (18+ MONTHS)
Gather several identical objects in a basket (e.g., blocks, balls, items from nature) and a tray that has the same number of compartments. Demonstrate how to take one object from the basket and place it into one of the compartments. Begin with just three objects, and progress to offering a larger tray and more objects as your child's skill improves. Older toddlers can also use tongs to transfer the objects.

JIGSAW PUZZLES (18+ MONTHS)

Toddlers of this age may be ready for their very first jigsaw puzzles. Start with just 2-piece puzzles to help your child find success in completing them, and then progress to offering puzzles with 3 pieces (or more) as they become more proficient. By the time your child is an older toddler, they may be capable of completing jigsaw puzzles with 12 to 24 pieces (or more).

OBJECT-TO-PICTURE MATCHING (18+ MONTHS)

Offer 5 to 7 objects from one category (e.g., figurines, household items, vehicles, items from nature), along with cards that are identical to the objects. Cards can either be purchased or DIY'd by taking photos of the objects, then printing and laminating them. As your toddler gains experience, you can begin offering cards that are similar, but not identical, to the object (e.g., a different color, model, or breed than the object).

STACKING PEG BOARD (18+ MONTHS)

This activity fosters your toddler's fine motor skills and hand-eye coordination but can also be used for learning colors and patterns and for sorting practice. Your child can stack the T-shaped pegs atop one another into the board in an endless array of combinations.

LOCK AND KEY (18+ MONTHS)

Offer your toddler a single lock and key in a tray (and tie the key to the tray for added safety). As your child's ability in successfully opening the lock progresses, you can offer several different locks and keys simultaneously so that your child is challenged to figure out which key belongs to each lock. A variation on this activity is to offer a locking coin box that requires a key to open.

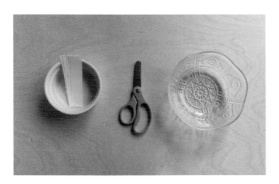

SCISSORS/CUTTING (2+ YEARS)
Start out with a pair of blunt-tipped safety scissors and small, thin strips of paper about ½-inch (1.25cm) wide. Show your toddler how to properly hold the scissors while making an open-and-close cutting motion. At first, offer your child unlined, blank paper strips for freely cutting off snippets. As their skill progresses, begin offering paper strips that have 3 to 4 bold, crosswise lines to practice cutting along.

THREADING (2+ YEARS)
Offer your toddler several pipe cleaners or stiff string (like natural hemp cording) and a bowl of dry pasta noodles, large pony beads, or cut straw pieces. Have your child practice threading the pieces onto the pipe cleaners (or string) one at a time. Tie a large knot at one end to prevent the pieces from sliding off.

MYSTERY BAG (2+ YEARS)
Help to hone your child's stereognostic sense by filling a loose drawstring bag with 5 to 10 objects that are easily able to be identified by touch alone. Invite your toddler to feel around inside the bag to identify various objects using only their sense of touch and to name it before pulling it out. Alternatively, you can ask them to find a specific object that you've named.

COLOR MATCHING (2+ YEARS)
Gather sample paint swatches in each of the following colors (two of each): red, yellow, blue, purple, green, orange, pink, black, brown, white, and gray. To begin, present to your child one swatch each of red, blue, and yellow while saying the name of the color: "This is red." Then invite your child to place the remaining swatches next to each of their matches. As your child masters the three primary colors, eventually include all of the colors.

HAMMERING (2+ YEARS)

Offer your child some modeling clay (or play dough), a few wooden pegs (or golf tees), and a wooden mallet, and watch the concentration begin! Your toddler will spend lots of time honing their hand-eye coordination and motor skills as they focus on successfully hammering all of the pegs into the clay one at a time.

SORTING (2.5+ YEARS)

Your toddler can develop an early understanding of mathematical concepts by sorting a bowl of small items (e.g., buttons, beans, counters, pom-poms) by a single quality (such as color or size) into different bowls or into a tray with multiple compartments.

PICTURE-TO-PICTURE MATCHING (2.5+ YEARS)

Offer your child a tray or basket containing 10 to 15 sets of matching photo cards. Divide the cards neatly into two piles. First, lay out all of the cards from one pile face up on the floor or table. Then invite your child to remove one card from the other pile, find its match on the floor or table, and place them together. Repeat until all cards are matched.

MATCHING ANIMAL HEADS AND TAILS (2.5+ YEARS)

This activity is set up just like picture-to-picture matching, except that the cards being used are the head and tail halves of photos depicting a variety of animals. One pile of cards (laid out) contains all of the animals' heads, while the other pile (being selected from) contains all of the animals' tails. To DIY this activity, print several animal photographs, and cut them into head and tail sections.

COUNTING BOARDS (2.5+ YEARS)

Once your toddler begins expressing an interest in numbers and counting, you can begin offering activities that provide practice with this skill. To use counting boards, invite your child to place wooden pegs into the holes next to each number, one at a time, while counting them aloud. This helps your child begin to understand the relationship between an abstract number symbol and the actual quantity it represents.

"I SPY" SOUND GAME (2.5+ YEARS)

When your child becomes interested in letters, sound games can help to develop their phonemic awareness, a necessary skill for reading. To play "I Spy," gather 3 to 4 familiar objects that each start with a different sound (for example, a ball, a toy tiger, and a pear). Then say, "I spy something beginning with /b/." (Say the "B" sound, not the name of the letter.) Invite your child to identify the ball.

PRESCHOOL ACTIVITIES

During the preschool years, your child will spend a great deal of time exploring the environment through movement and purposeful activity, further developing many skills that were initially learned in the first three years. This section includes a blend of traditional Montessori and Montessori-inspired activities that are appropriate for children from three to six years old. Remember that all children develop on their own timeline, so your preschooler may be ready sooner for some activities than others. (Note: these activities are only intended as a supplement to the home environment and not as a formal homeschool curriculum.)

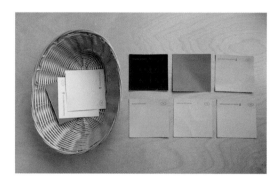

COLOR GRADING
Gather a set of 5 to 7 color swatches of a single color that vary in shade (e.g., dark green to light green), and lay them out randomly in front of your child. Show your child the darkest and lightest swatches, and then invite your child to place all of the swatches in order from darkest to lightest. Repeat with shades of red, orange, yellow, blue, and purple.

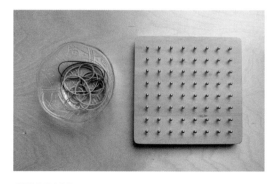

GEOBOARD
Encourage your child to practice fine-motor skills and manual dexterity by stretching elastic bands across the pegs of a geoboard. Initially, your child will work on mastering the movements required to stretch the bands across the pegs to create their own free-form patterns. As their skill progresses, they can try to match specific patterns on cards or create more complicated patterns of their own.

FABRIC MATCHING

Gather 5 to 7 sets of matching fabric squares and divide them into two piles. Lay out all of the fabric squares from one pile on the floor. Working one fabric square at a time, invite your child to use their sense of touch to find the matching square on the floor and place them together. For an added challenge, invite your child to do this activity while blindfolded.

SOUND MATCHING

Fill 4 to 6 matching pairs of opaque jars with materials that make different sounds when shaken, like dried beans, a small bell, pebbles, rice, etc. Invite your child to choose a jar and listen to its sound while shaken, then shake each of the remaining jars to identify its match. This is an easy activity to DIY using empty spice jars that you've painted black.

RHYMING WORDS

Gather 5 to 7 pairs of household objects or toys whose names rhyme with one another (e.g., dino and rhino, bell and shell, duck and truck). Invite your child to match the rhyming objects. Alternatively, take turns coming up with a word and asking each other to think of a rhyming word.

CATEGORIES

Gather 5 to 7 pairs of objects or toys (or pictures) that belong to the same category, such as an apple and banana (fruit), pants and shirt (clothing), or cow and pig figurines (animals). Separate the matching objects into two piles on the floor. Invite your child to choose an object from one pile and find its match in the other pile. (This activity can also be offered using photo cards in lieu of actual objects.)

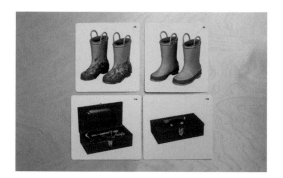

OPPOSITES

Present your child with 10 to 15 pairs of cards featuring photos that are opposites of one another (e.g., full and empty, open and closed, clean and dirty). Separate the pairs into two piles, then lay out one of the piles on the floor. Invite your child to choose a card from the existing pile and find its match on the floor. (The cards can either be purchased commercially or DIY'd by printing at home.)

SOUND BLENDING GAME

Gather 3 to 5 familiar objects (or pictures) that have only 2 or 3 sounds in their names (e.g., cup, box, pen). Say the name of each object aloud. Then say, "I'm thinking of one of these items. I'll give you a hint—listen closely! It's the . . ." Then choose an object, and say its name by sounding out the individual letters: "/c/ . . . /u/ . . . /p/." Then invite your child to identify the object.

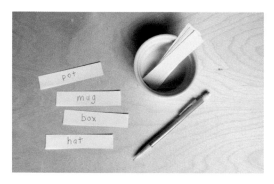

SECRET MESSAGES GAME

Tell your child (with an air of secrecy, to make it fun) that you're going to write a secret message just for them. Write the name of a household object on a slip of paper ("No peeking!"), and then invite your child to read it silently. Ask them to find the object with that name and place the label on it. Start with easy words like "box" or "mug," and increase the challenge as they're ready.

ACTIVITY WORDS GAME

Write several action words on little slips of paper (e.g., jump, sit, spin, hop, clap), and invite your child to choose one. Your child reads the slip of paper silently and acts it out while you guess the action, just like charades. Be sure to take turns with your child to amp up the fun factor!

AUDIOBOOKS

Provide your child with a pair of headphones, an audiobook (on a digital MP3 player), and, if desired, the actual physical book to use for reading along. Audiobooks for preschoolers can either be purchased online or recorded yourself using your own books at home. Just don't forget to include a special sound that indicates when to turn the page if using along with a physical book.

THREE-PART CARDS

Your child can learn new vocabulary words for any topic of interest by matching separate "picture cards" and "label cards" to a set of "control cards" that contain both. The control cards are laid out first, then the pictures are matched to the control cards, and finally the labels are matched to the pictures. For a greater challenge, your child can begin by matching the pictures with the labels, then check their work using the control cards.

SAND TRAY

Pour a thin layer of craft sand into any shallow tray of a highly contrasting color. Begin by inviting your child to explore by drawing basic shapes and lines. When your child eventually begins to show an interest in writing, invite them to practice tracing the alphabet letters in the sand. Be sure to show your child how to erase their writing in the tray by gently shaking it from side to side.

"BRING ME" GAME

This activity bolsters your child's early math skills, as it combines large movement with an easy, hands-on way to practice counting. Ask your child to retrieve a particular number of objects from around your home. For example, "Bring me 5 blue blocks," or "Bring me 3 spoons." Your child must keep the number in their mind while they retrieve the objects and bring them back to you.

CARDS AND COUNTERS

In this activity, your child can practice the skill of counting quantities up to 10. Prepare a tray containing numeral cards from 1 to 10 and a basket of 55 counters (e.g., any small objects that are identical, such as vase-filler gems). Your child should first place the numeral cards in order from left to right, then place the appropriate number of counters underneath each numeral card in rows of two.

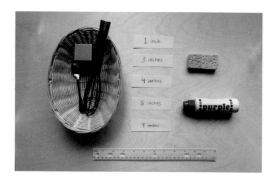

USING A RULER

Offer your child a basket of 4 to 5 objects that have varying even lengths, a set of measurement labels that each correspond to only one object, and a metric ruler. Lay out the measurement labels, and then select one object from the basket. The ruler is placed underneath the object, carefully lining up the left edges. Then find the measurement on the ruler. Finally, the object and corresponding measurement label are matched together.

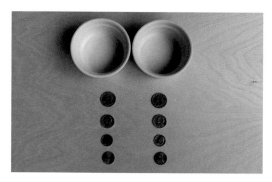

COIN MATCHING

Gather together 2 of each type of coin. Place one from each pair into two bowls. Lay out coins from the first bowl in a column on the table. Remove a coin from the second bowl and look for its match from the first set of coins. Match all of the remaining coins in the same way. (Note: names of different coins aren't necessary for this activity but can be introduced at a later time.)

DAILY CALENDAR

An excellent way to help your child begin to grasp the abstract concept of the passage of time is to maintain a daily calendar. Your child can take on the responsibility of adjusting the calendar each day to reflect the proper month and date, season, moon phase, current weather, holidays, or any other special events. Using a calendar also helps to reinforce your child's mathematical and executive functioning skills.

SEQUENCING LIFE CYCLES

Studying the unique life cycle of various plants, animals, and other organisms can really help to open a child's eyes to the wonders of our planet. Offer your child a linear (or circular) representation of a specific life cycle, along with the corresponding photos (or figurines) to place in order at each stage. You can also read a children's nonfiction book pertaining to the life cycle to aid their understanding.

SPROUTING SEEDS

Help your child learn about plant growth in a hands-on way by germinating seeds together! Fill a Mason jar about three-quarters full with potting mix, add 2 to 3 large seeds (e.g., peas or beans), top with another inch of potting mix, and lightly water. Keep it in a warm place, and observe the seeds each day over the course of the next week or two, adding water when necessary.

LIVING VS. NON-LIVING

Prepare a tray containing a basket of 5 to 7 items (figurines or photos) to represent either living or non-living things and a piece of paper with a T-chart drawn ("Living" and "Non-Living"). Name each category for your child. Explain that living organisms use energy, grow and develop, reproduce, respond to their environment, and adapt. Then invite your child to sort the items under the proper column according to whether they are living or non-living.

MAGNETIC VS. NON-MAGNETIC

Prepare a tray containing a magnet, a basket of 10 to 15 items that are either magnetic or non-magnetic (e.g., paper clip, key, eraser, button, etc.), and a piece of paper with a T-chart drawn ("Magnetic" and "Non-Magnetic"). Name each category for your child, and then invite them to use the magnet to determine which items are magnetic, sorting them under the proper column. Older children can be challenged to predict ahead of time.

PLANTS VS. ANIMALS

Prepare a tray containing a basket of 5 to 7 items (figurines or photos) to represent either plants or animals, and a piece of paper with a T-chart drawn ("Plants" and "Animals"). Name each category for your child. Invite your child to sort the items under the proper column according to whether they are a plant or animal.

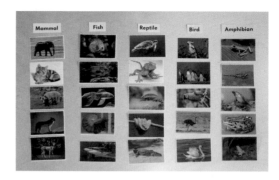

CLASSIFYING VERTEBRATE ANIMALS

Offer your child a basket of 20 to 25 photos to represent either fish, birds, reptiles, amphibians, or mammals, as well as a label for each category. Place the labels in a row in front of your child, and name each of them. Briefly describe to your child the primary characteristics that define each group. Then invite your child to sort the items under the proper labels according to which vertebrate class they belong to.

SINK OR FLOAT

Prepare a tray containing a basket of 10 to 15 small objects that either sink or float, a bowl of water, and a piece of laminated paper with a T-chart drawn ("Sink" and "Float"). Name each category for your child, then invite them to use the bowl of water to figure out which items sink or float, sorting them under the proper column. Older children can be challenged to predict ahead of time.

CLASSICAL MUSIC APPRECIATION

Compositions such as *Peter and the Wolf* or *Swan Lake* are engaging stories that can be used to begin introducing classical music to preschoolers. Simply set up a listening area for your child, or combine with a matching activity using photos and figurines of the instruments being played. Older children can also tackle more in-depth studies of the life and times of the work and composer.

COLOR MIXING

This activity helps to reinforce your child's understanding of how primary colors can be mixed to produce secondary colors. Offer your child a plate containing three small glasses filled halfway with water, three dropper bottles containing red, blue, and yellow water, and a small spoon. Invite your child to add 5 drops of each colored water to the glass between them, then use the spoon to stir and observe the color produced.

PIN PUNCHING

Draw a simple shape (e.g., circle, triangle, heart) with a thin black marker on a square of construction paper, and place it on top of a cork trivet. Invite your child to use a jumbo push pin to carefully make many small holes in the paper along the line, pricking repeatedly until the shape is effectively "cut out" from the paper by all of the holes.

YOGA CARDS

Offer opportunities for gross-motor movement by providing a child-sized yoga mat and a basket containing 5 to 9 picture cards of various whole-body yoga poses. Rotate the available cards on a regular basis. This activity can be done together with a parent or independently if your child prefers. Yoga cards for children can either be purchased or DIY'd by taking photos of your child doing the poses, then printing and laminating.

BOARD GAMES

Playing simple board games is a wonderful way to help a preschool-aged child cultivate emotional development, creative problem solving, and essential social skills, such as turn-taking and cooperation. Many games are also designed to help your child learn basic concepts, such as colors, shapes, counting, and matching, among others.

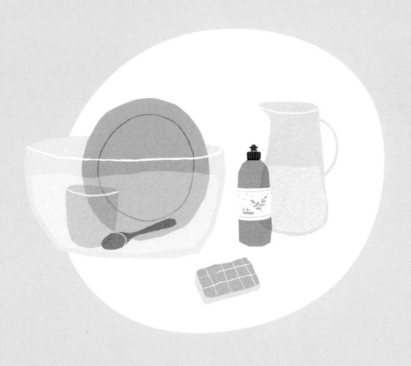

THROUGHOUT THE HOME

BUILDING PRACTICAL LIFE SKILLS

Children are keen observers of everything they see happening in their environment, especially at home. They see us wiping tables, cleaning windows, sweeping, folding laundry, and washing dishes, and quite naturally, they seek to imitate us. They have an innate desire to be involved in our daily activities, often from a much earlier age than we may even realize. And it was Dr. Maria Montessori who recognized one of the young child's greatest inner needs: "Help me to do it alone."

Practical life activities in a Montessori environment are all the things that we do each day to look after ourselves and our homes. As your child's independence is such an important goal in Montessori, it's essential to help your child learn how to manage their own personal care and make valuable contributions to the well-being of your family's home environment.

As adults, we tend to focus on the end product of our tasks—the clean table, the shiny window, or the neatly folded laundry pile. However, our children's primary point of interest is in the process itself—the wiping motions, the mechanics of using a

spray bottle, and the sorting and folding of each sock or shirt. Participating in these tasks scaffolds your child's ability to assume responsibility, develops concentration and a sense of order, engages them in repetition, refines their coordination and motor skills, indirectly prepares them for the later learning of language and math, and offers the experience of completing a full cycle of activity.

As your child grows, they will begin to master various skills, and you may find that their interest in them begins to wane. It's important to anticipate how you can prepare your child's environment to offer opportunities for involvement in tasks of increasing complexity so that they feel challenged enough in their work to remain engaged and interested. In this chapter, we will explore several examples of age-appropriate practical life skills to consider incorporating into your child's routine at home during their early years. Just remember to keep your mind open to the many other possibilities that exist based on your family's own unique values and culture at home.

INTRODUCING PRACTICAL LIFE TO INFANTS

While very young infants cannot independently participate in most practical life activities, they are still collaboratively involved as we assist them in completing tasks, such as changing a diaper, taking a bath, getting dressed, and eating. However, instead of doing these things *to* our babies, as if they have no ideas or opinions about what's being done to them, it is a better approach to reframe our perspective as one of completing these tasks *with* our babies, always remaining aware and respectful of their experience as human beings. Instead of *getting our child dressed*, we are *helping them learn to get dressed*. There is a distinct difference in this mentality!

During the earliest months, calmly letting your infant know what you're about to do ("I'm going to help you get your shirt on now!") and then speaking to them directly about the process as it occurs ("First, I'm going to pull this shirt over your head. Next, I'm going to help you put your arm into this hole . . .") is an important first step in respectfully communicating this mutual partnership to your infant. As your child's motor skills improve,

you can gradually give them greater control over each process, inasmuch as their abilities will allow. For example, when you recognize that your infant is actually beginning to push their own arms through the shirt holes, allow them to take ownership over this action. By doing so, you are gradually helping your infant learn how to dress themselves.

As your infant becomes capable of sitting independently, their hands are essentially freed for new tasks that were not possible before, including a greater level of independence with practical life activities. Activities that are appropriate to introduce to infants under the age of 12 months (depending on your child's individual motor skills) might include the following:

- Offering a child-sized fork, spoon, and cup to practice using at mealtimes while you model eating alongside them using your own utensils.

- After your infant finishes a meal or if a small spill occurs, offering a small washcloth so they can "help" to wipe the table.

- During diaper changes, inviting them to retrieve a clean diaper and wipes before you begin and to discard the soiled diaper into the appropriate receptacle afterward.

- While doing dishes, inviting your infant to remove clean dishes from the drying rack and hand them to you to store away (or store themselves, if they are capable).

- Inviting your infant to help you fill a pet's bowl with food and/or water.

- Showing your older infant how to dust the leaves of a houseplant with a cloth or water using a small pitcher.

One hallmark of the Montessori approach, especially with regard to practical life work, is to provide real, child-sized furniture and tools that a child can handle with ease. Dr. Montessori noted time and again that the young children in her classrooms were better able to achieve independence and success in their tasks when they had tools that were appropriately sized for their hands and bodies.

Some of the essential child-sized items to consider including in your home environment are a table, chair, utensils, and cup for mealtimes; a sponge, brush, and washcloths for wiping and cleaning; a broom and dustpan for sweeping; a watering can, mister, and/or gardening tools for plant care; a learning tower and child-sized kitchen utensils for food preparation; low hooks on the wall for hanging a coat or for storing other tools; and a step stool to help your child reach an adult-height bathroom sink. There are also many other kinds of child-sized tools and furniture available for all manners of practical life purposes, depending on your family's culture and lifestyle.

Young children are highly adaptable to their environments and will almost always figure out a way to make it work, so don't let it stop you if your child's current set of tools aren't child-sized. However, should you wish to invest in any child-sized items for your home, the "Montessori Furniture & Materials" section contains several suggestions for where they can be purchased.

PRACTICAL LIFE FOR TODDLERS

CARE OF SELF

Personal Hygiene

Handwashing, toothbrushing, hairbrushing, nose wiping, and toileting are all self-care activities in which toddlers can actively participate shortly after their first birthday. Provide your child with a step stool to independently access the sink (or a low area with a washing basin), and make sure all materials they need for each task are easily located within their reach.

Modeling for your child as you do these activities together is helpful as they can observe how to perform each step. Allow your toddler to move slowly at their own pace. Although you can certainly guide your toddler's hands in the beginning, be sure to step back to let them take over as soon as you sense their efforts to do it alone.

Activities like handwashing, in particular, will often get a bit messy during the initial stages of learning, so keep a dry towel handy for accidental messes, and show your child how to clean up when they are finished. (More detailed information on these topics is located in "The Bathroom" chapter of this book.)

Independent Dressing

Sometime between the age of about 15 to 18 months, toddlers typically begin showing an interest in dressing themselves. They are also capable of choosing their own clothing from a limited selection of two choices that you've provided (e.g., the red or the blue shirt). Your toddler will appreciate having opportunities to practice getting dressed independently, including putting on their own underwear, shirt/dress, pants/shorts/skirt, socks, and shoes (slip-ons or with Velcro fasteners). Your child will require lots of practice over many months before becoming truly proficient, so it's important that they are given practice with these tasks every day.

Model slowly at first as you help your child get dressed, with your child sitting in front of you and their back facing you, instead of being face to face. It is much easier for your toddler to see how to properly hold and put on their clothing from this perspective. Once they begin attempting to get dressed on their own, remain quiet and patient even as they struggle a bit. Resist the urge to intervene unless your child explicitly asks for help. If your child sounds as if they are on the verge of becoming overly frustrated and giving up altogether, then you can offer a gentle verbal reminder that you are available if they'd like your help. If they do ask for help, don't take over and do everything for your child. Doing so inadvertently communicates the message that you believe they are incapable and that you can do it better. Instead, only offer a bit of help with a small step of the process (e.g., hold a pant leg out), and then allow them to proceed independently again.

You can teach your toddler a little rhyming phrase to remember how to put on their pants: "Tag on the ground, feet in the holes, wiggle them up until you see your toes . . . then stand up, and pull it up over the bum!"

The process of dressing takes a lot longer when your toddler is still learning, so if you have a strict time schedule for school or work to which you must adhere, then try to budget in some extra time in the mornings and evenings for this process to occur at your child's pace.

The Montessori "Coat Flip"

Putting on a coat to go outside is a task that your toddler can easily learn to do on their own from about the age of 18 months by using the Montessori coat flip! Start by having your child place their open coat on the floor faceup in front of them so that the tag is directly in front of their toes. Next, your child should bend down to place their hands in the armholes, and as they stand up, they will swing the coat up and over their head such that their arms naturally slide into the arms and the coat falls perfectly into position. You can also teach your toddler a little rhyming phrase to accompany the steps to help them remember how to do it: "Tag by my toes, hands in the holes, swing it up, and over it goes!"

Dressing Frames

If your toddler shows an interest in learning how to use the various fasteners found on items of clothing, you might consider offering an opportunity to practice with Montessori dressing frames. Start with simpler ones, like snaps or Velcro, and gradually progress to more difficult frames, like zippers, large buttons, and laces. Only offer one or two at a time for your child to work on, and provide lots of opportunity for practice and mastery before presenting others. While dressing frames can be purchased, you can also simply hang items of your child's clothing (e.g., coats or shirts with buttons, snaps, or zippers) on the back of a small chair and allow your toddler to practice that way.

Helping with Laundry

Even the youngest of toddlers will show great interest and enthusiasm in assisting as you do the laundry. Invite your child to help you put clothes in the washer and take clothes out of the dryer or hang them on a drying rack or line. You can also show them how to add soap, choose settings, and turn knobs or press

buttons. Once the laundry is done, involve your toddler as you sort, fold, and put away clothing. You can also invite your toddler to help match up the socks for you.

Food Preparation

Seeing, hearing, touching, smelling, and, of course, tasting various foods while making a snack or assisting in the preparation of your family's meals will easily engage all of your toddler's senses at once. It's no wonder that they love to be involved in the kitchen! Here are some ideas for simple activities to try with your child in this area of practical life, based on your own observations of their individual readiness:

- adding ingredients to a bowl or blender
- filling a steamer basket with vegetables (or dumplings)
- pouring and mixing premeasured ingredients
- spreading butter/jam/cream cheese onto crackers or bread
- banana peeling and slicing (with a blunt spreading knife or banana slicer)
- cutting fruits and vegetables (with a wavy chopper)
- mashing an avocado or potatoes
- cracking eggs into a bowl
- egg peeling and slicing (with an egg slicer)
- orange peeling
- orange juicing (with a small manual juicer)
- spice grinding (with a mortar and pestle)
- potato washing and scrubbing
- rinsing berries or lettuce greens (in a colander)
- making a smoothie
- removing strawberry tops
- pouring a drink (water, milk, or juice)

CARE OF ENVIRONMENT

General Housework

As your child begins showing interest in the tasks you're completing around your home, extend an invitation to your child to help in whatever capacity they can. How much they will be able to contribute will depend on how old your child is and their individual level of skill, so this will necessarily differ from child to child.

Your child's safety should be your top priority, so you'll want to prevent your child from becoming involved in any tasks that may have a potential to cause injury (e.g., your toddler shouldn't be allowed to put away the dinner knives). However, as long as there is adult supervision, most activities are fairly safe for your child.

Remain patient and try to refrain from correcting your child's mistakes as they are learning. If there is an accident or spill, treat it as a learning opportunity, and gently show your child how to clean up, without scolding or punishment.

Whenever possible, provide your toddler with smaller tools that are scaled to their size and proportions so that they're more likely to be successful in completing the task on their own. It is quite easy nowadays to find mini versions of many ordinary tools (e.g., dustpans, cutting boards, gardening tools), although there are some that are simple enough to make yourself (e.g., cutting a regular-sized dish sponge in half to create two smaller sponges).

An added bonus is that doing daily chores *alongside* your child (as opposed to trying to distract them as you rush to do it all by yourself) creates more time and opportunity to build genuine connections with your child. That's a win-win for everyone!

Here are some easy ideas for involving your toddler in common housework tasks:

- **Washing dishes:** Wash dishes and silverware with a small sponge in a small basin of water, and place them into a drying rack; load dishes into a dishwasher; empty and put away clean plates, cups, and bowls from a dishwasher; sort clean silverware into a utensil tray.

- **Dusting, sweeping, and mopping:** Clean using a small feather duster or dusting cloth, a mini dustpan and hand broom, a child-sized push broom or mop, or a Swiffer sweeper that has been made child-sized (by removing the extension poles).

- **Window washing:** Use a miniature spray bottle (filled with just water or a water/vinegar mixture) to lightly spray a window,

wipe in downward strokes with a small squeegee, and dry excess water with a cloth.

- **Table washing:** Use a small washcloth and a bucket of water to clean a low table surface (e.g., their weaning table).

- **Table setting and clearing:** Set the table for snack time or a family meal. (Use a placemat with outlined spaces for all necessary items marked: plate, cup, fork, knife, spoon, and napkin.) At the end of a meal, clear dishes from the table, and place them in a designated area for dirty items (i.e., sink or dishwasher).

- **Folding napkins or cloths:** Use several plain napkins or washcloths that have proper folding lines drawn (or sewn) onto them to practice basic folding techniques.

- **Pet care:** Scoop and pour food and water into the appropriate bowls for pets; help to take pets outside for short walks with an adult. (Note: pets can sometimes be unpredictable, so always remain present, supervise, and exercise proper discretion during these activities to help keep your child safe.)

- **Plant care:** Gently clean the leaves of houseplants with a small, damp sponge; water plants with a small watering can or plant mister; harvest any edible fruits (or remove dead leaves) from a plant; assist in tending a larger outdoor garden. (Note: for safety, keep any potentially toxic plants out of your child's reach.)

TRANSFER WORK

Most practical life work can be organically integrated into your daily activities around the home, so it very often won't require the use of a tray on the shelf. However, there is one kind of practical life exercise that can greatly benefit from being organized into a shallow tray for your child: transfer work. These are the activities that involve your child in learning how to carefully and precisely pour and transfer different materials from one container to another using various kinds of tools. Organizing the materials for transfer work into a tray is not just for the purposes of order and presentation but also to help contain the inevitable spills that will occur as your child explores and refines their skills.

The following activities are offered with suggested ages for introduction; however, these are intended only as general guidelines. Be sure to spend some time observing your child's interests and skills before introducing an activity to decide if it is safe and appropriate.

- **Moving large items by hand** (13+ months): Your child uses their hand to transfer several medium to large items (e.g., balls, pom-poms, wooden blocks) from one bowl to another and then back again.

- **Spooning large items** (13+ months): Your child uses a soup spoon or kitchen ladle to transfer medium to large items from one bowl to another and back again.

- **Dry pouring** (16+ months): Your child pours dry materials (e.g., beans, rice, corn kernels) from one small cup or pitcher to another slowly and carefully to minimize spilling and then back again.

- **Wet pouring** (16+ months): Your child first pours water from one cup (or a small spouted pitcher) to another and back again. As their skill progresses, they pour water from a pitcher to a cup. Finally, they pour water from a pitcher to several smaller glasses without spilling or overpouring.

- **Dry objects with various utensils** (18+ months): Your child picks up and transfers objects (e.g., pom-poms, small sponge pieces, and other easily grabbed items) from one bowl to another and back again using various kinds of utensils that progress in difficulty (e.g., small ice or bread tongs, child-sized kitchen tongs, chopsticks, jumbo tweezers, and regular tweezers).

- **Spooning/scooping small items** (18+ months): Your child uses a small spoon or scoop to transfer small dry materials (e.g., beans, rice, or corn kernels) from one bowl to another and back again.

- **Wet materials** (18+ months): Your child uses a kitchen ladle, deep soup spoon, or slotted spoon to transfer wet materials like ice cubes or water beads from one bowl to another and back again.

- **Using a sponge** (2+ years): Your child uses a child-sized sponge to soak up and squeeze water from one bowl to another.

- **Using a turkey baster** (2.5+ years): Your child uses a short turkey baster to transfer water from one bowl to another.

- **Using an eyedropper** (2.5+ years): Your child uses an eyedropper to transfer water from one cup to another.

PRACTICAL LIFE FOR PRESCHOOLERS

CARE OF SELF

Making the Bed

It is simple enough to show your child how to pull a blanket or comforter over the mattress properly and place the pillow near the head, such that their bed looks neat and presentable. While their execution of this process may not look perfect (or even remotely close to your demonstration), it is the effort they make that truly counts. Encourage your child to establish this habit each morning before leaving their bedroom for breakfast. Over time, their skill will improve.

Using Clothespins

If your family already uses a drying rack or line for hanging laundry to dry, then be sure to involve your preschooler in using clothespins to help with this task. And even if you use a dryer instead, your child can still learn how to use clothespins for fine-motor benefits as a standalone shelf activity. Simply present your child with a small basket of 10 to 20 clothespins, and invite them to pin each clothespin, one at a time, around the edge of the basket until all of them have been used. They can then unpin all of the clothespins and place them back into the basket.

Sewing

Sewing is a wonderful life skill for your child to learn from a young age. Provide your preschooler with a large, blunt darning needle that you've prethreaded with embroidery floss or yarn. Tie a large knot at the end of the thread. Offer a small embroidery hoop fitted with burlap or embroidery fabric (or a small "plastic canvas" card, typically sold in craft stores), and allow your child to freely experiment with sewing. As your child's skill improves, you can draw shapes and patterns on the fabric for them to follow. You can also show your child how to thread the needle and tie a knot on their own, sew a large button onto fabric, and eventually create small projects, such as sewing a small pillow.

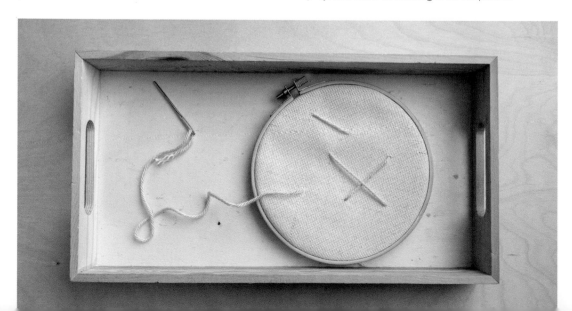

Braiding

Your child can easily learn how to braid using simple materials. Tie three differently colored, thick shoelaces or cotton cords to the top of a clipboard. (Or use binder clips to secure at the top of a thick piece of cardboard.) Demonstrate how to interlace the cord colors to create the braid (e.g., yellow over red, then blue over yellow, etc.). Allow your child plenty of opportunity to practice.

Using Office Supplies

With a proper demonstration and adult supervision until their skill becomes established, a preschool-aged child is capable of using a variety of office supplies, such as a hole puncher, clear tape, paper clips, binder clips, envelopes, a pencil sharpener, and a stapler, for their arts-and-crafts projects.

Food Preparation

- **Apple slicing:** Use an apple slicer/corer to cut an apple into slices. (This takes a lot of strength, so in the beginning, an adult may need to scaffold this task by pushing the slicer into the apple partway before allowing the child to finish.)

- **Peeling and chopping vegetables:** Assist with peeling vegetables that have a thin skin, such as carrots or cucumbers, using a Y-shaped peeler; chop vegetables with a child-sized nylon chef's knife.

- **Toasting bread:** Insert slices of bread into a pop-up toaster or toaster oven; adjust time and temperature settings (with adult assistance).

- **Assembling a sandwich:** Spread nut butters, jams, butter, mashed avocado, or other condiments onto slices of bread; add lettuce greens, cheese slices, and/or deli meats.

- **Measuring ingredients:** Pour liquids to a definitively marked line on a liquid measuring cup; use a dry measuring spoon or cup to scoop dry ingredients, then level off with the back of a butter knife.

- **Baking:** With minimal adult assistance or by following a simple visual recipe—gather, measure, and mix together all ingredients for baked goods, then scoop into a muffin tin (or pour into a cake pan, roll into a ball and place onto a cookie sheet, etc.).

- **Cooking with heat:** With adult supervision, safely use an electric hot plate or skillet on a low setting to cook simple foods, like scrambled eggs and pancakes.

CARE OF ENVIRONMENT

Flower Arranging

Young children genuinely appreciate beauty in their environment, and they also enjoy being able to contribute to the creation of that beauty. Prepare a tray containing a small vase, a child-sized pitcher of water, a funnel, several fresh-cut flower stems, and a small sponge. Then invite your child to use the funnel to pour water into the vase and arrange the flower stems in it however they would like. (The sponge can be used to soak up any spilled drops of water.) Your child can then place the flower arrangement in a spot of their choice in your home for the enjoyment of others, such as on a sideboard, end table, weaning table, or the family dining table.

Tending a Garden

Beyond the simple watering and trimming of a single plant, a preschooler is typically excited about the prospect of gaining more responsibility by assisting in the maintenance of a larger garden. If you're limited on available green space, then even a small container garden on a balcony or front doorstep will help to excite your child's curiosity about nature and the life cycle of plants. While flowers are beautiful and a great addition to any garden, don't forget to include some fruits and vegetables, too! This will encourage your

child to try foods that they may have otherwise been reluctant to eat and can also serve as a natural springboard for conversations about where their food comes from. Invite your child to participate in the care of the garden in any way that they are interested and capable, from watering to composting, weeding, trimming, and harvesting. Whenever possible, try to make real, child-sized gardening tools available for use, including some of the essentials, like a trowel, garden fork, rake, watering can, and gardening gloves.

Polishing Wood

A preschool-aged child is also ready for more steps in the sequence of an activity than is typically offered in preliminary exercises, like pouring or spooning. A great way to engage your child in an activity requiring more sequencing awareness and concentration is by offering a wood-polishing activity. Prepare a tray containing a small bowl of all-natural, nontoxic wood polish (such as Daddy Van's brand), any wooden object to be polished (e.g., kitchen spoon, carved animal figurine, an old baby teether, etc.), and two soft cotton cloths. Demonstrate for your child how to gently apply a small amount of polish to the object using the first cloth, and then how to use the second cloth to buff the object until finished. Finish by inviting your child to help clean up by wiping out the polish bowl and placing the used cotton cloths into the laundry bin.

Using Real Tools

While there are many pretend toy versions of actual tools available for children, it is better to offer a child-sized version of the real thing.

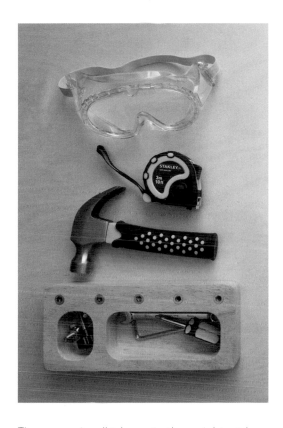

They are naturally drawn to the weight and feel of a real measuring tape or screwdriver and the heft of an actual hammer in their hand as they learn how to safely hammer real metal nails. Under adult supervision and while wearing safety goggles to protect their eyes, invite your child to practice their hammering skills on an old piece of wood (or into a fresh pumpkin during the fall season). You can also encourage your child to practice measuring objects and furniture around your home and outside using a measuring tape. A graded bolt board is also helpful in assisting your child in developing their hand-eye coordination as they learn the practical skill of using a screwdriver.

GRACE AND COURTESY

It isn't a novel concept that social skills and polite behavior are things that children must learn over time. However, this aspect tends to be overlooked until a child has done something socially inappropriate, at which point an adult may decide to step in to offer a correction. And in doing so, the hope is that the child will remember the incident and alter their behavior in the future.

However, this is a *reactive response* to a mere lack of social skills, and it isn't nearly as effective as a *proactive approach* that will actually help your child learn these skills *before* they are expected to use them in real-life situations.

There are two primary ways that you can help your child learn proper social behavior: through modeling and role-playing.

To begin with, there is a lot to be said for modeling. You are your child's first teacher. They will absorb and take on as their own whatever phrases and behaviors they see and hear coming from you, not only in your interactions with others but also in their own interactions with you. So if you are expecting your child to say "please" and "thank you," the best place to start is by saying "please" and "thank you" at every appropriate opportunity when talking to, or in front of, your child. The converse of this also holds true. If there are undesirable phrases or behaviors that your child is expressing in social situations—or any skills that are entirely lacking—you might first ask yourself if these things were inadvertently learned from you or someone else in your home or that perhaps they aren't being modeled at all. If this is the case, your first step in addressing the situation should be to change your own behavior. (Or have a chat with any other individuals in your home who may be modeling the inappropriate behavior.)

Role-playing is another simple but very effective way for your child to learn and practice using positive social skills before actually needing them. These are brief, one-on-one sessions between you and your child (or even better, with siblings, if you have more than one child) where you practice socially acceptable behavior as if it were actually happening. These opportunities are incredibly helpful for young children, who do not yet have the myriad life experiences that we do as adults so that they can practice what they *should* do in a neutral, no-pressure environment. The more they practice, the quicker they will be able to recall and properly use those skills in a real-life situation.

While there are many possibilities for grace and courtesy lessons beyond the scope of this book, and especially some that may be specific to your culture and community, here are just a few ideas for common scenarios that could be considered essential skills for any child:

Greeting a Guest

Tell your child that you are going to show them how to greet someone and that they will be able to practice with you. Face your child and say, "Hello, how are you?" Then ask your child to say, "I am well, thank you. How are you?" After they say this, reply, "I am also well, thank you." If there are other children present, practice this with each child. Once all children have had a chance to practice with you, invite them to practice with one another.

Saying "Excuse Me"

Explain that when you need to get somewhere but someone is in your way, you should say, "Excuse me." Tell them that you are going to practice saying "Excuse me." Have another person (an older child or adult) stand somewhere close by that would make them an obstacle in your path (e.g., in a narrow hall or doorway). Walk toward the other person, and when you get to where they are, say, "Excuse me." The other person then moves to the side to allow you to pass. Switch roles and invite your child to be the one who is walking and needs to say, "Excuse me."

Politely Interrupting

Explain that you are going to demonstrate how to politely interrupt an adult who is busy talking to someone else. Invite two other people (two adults or an adult and an older child) to begin talking to one another, then approach them quietly. Gently place your hand on the adult's shoulder and wait until they turn to look at you. Say, "Excuse me . . ." and ask a simple question. Listen carefully to the adult's response, then say "Thank you," and walk away. Switch roles to allow your child to practice politely interrupting. (This technique is also known as "the waiting hand," which is easy for children to remember when they need a reminder to do this in the future.)

THE GREAT OUTDOORS
CONNECTING WITH NATURE

Our children are born explorers. From the moment of birth, a newborn begins using all of their senses to learn about the world, from the familiar smell of their caregivers, to the sweet taste of milk, the feel of a soft blanket on their skin, and the sights and sounds of their home environment. When taken outside on a warm and sunny day, a baby will delight in the sensation of soft grass tickling their feet and be content to watch the branches of a tree gently swaying in the breeze. They have an innate appreciation for such minutia, often overlooked by the busy adult for whom such fine details have faded into the background of life.

Dr. Montessori recognized that young children have a deep sense of connection with nature and tasked the adult with helping to maintain that connection by not only providing children with tools made of natural materials to work with but also lots of time to play and explore outside. A toddler's greatly improved motor skills and ability to walk independently frees their hands to experiment with the natural world on their own terms. And as they reach the preschool years, they will enjoy and take pride in helping to take care of their environment.

Our role during these early years is to focus on letting go a bit—to allow our child to get dirty, play in the rain, quite literally stop and the smell the roses, investigate a line of ants on the sidewalk, and climb trees in a grand effort to see the world from another perspective.

In this chapter, we'll learn how to create more opportunities *outside* of the home that will help to cultivate your child's connection with nature and foster their burgeoning sense of responsibility around environmental stewardship.

INFANTS

SENSORIAL EXPERIENCES

An infant's primary means of gaining information about the world is through their senses. Their absorbent mind is taking in everything at once—all of the sights, sounds, smells, textures, and tastes that define their environment. Thus, your baby's first experiences with the natural world need not be extravagant, as it is all very new and stimulating for them.

The first couple of weeks following birth should be spent at home in a relatively calm and quiet environment that fosters a gentle transition to the world outside of the womb. Newborns are not born with fully developed vision, having a focusing distance of about 8 to 10 inches (20–25cm). They will usually squint when brought outside into daylight, which is a bit too bright for them during this early time. However, this isn't to say that your baby cannot be brought outside, as they certainly can! It's just that your newborn will be less able to appreciate the sights and instead focus more on the smells, sounds, and physical sensations of nature.

By the time your infant is three to four months old, they will be eager and happy to explore the world outside. But their experiences should not be limited to the confines of a stroller or carrier. Freedom of movement is essential! Begin by bringing a soft blanket outside for your baby to lay on in the grass. Let their tiny feet hang off the edge just a bit so they can feel the grass in their toes. Alternatively, you can place them close enough to the edge of the blanket so that they can see and feel the grass with their hands during tummy time.

You can also try placing your baby on their back under a shady tree, allowing them to watch the branches and leaves as they sway in the breeze. You can also bring along a favorite toy or two, and simply allow your baby to play freely on the blanket in the warm sunshine. Just be mindful that they are wearing sunscreen and do not overheat, or set them up in a shady spot if the sun is too intense that day.

As your baby becomes capable of sitting independently and crawling, allow them to explore beyond the edges of a blanket. Most infants find great enjoyment in crawling through the grass, provided that it is a safe space to do so. You might even gather a few natural items from outside for your baby to explore, such as a small rock, pine cone, stick, leaves, and a flower. A nature-themed "treasure basket" activity that includes these kinds of items can also be offered indoors.

A common, legitimate concern for most parents is what to do if their baby puts something into their mouth, such as a stick, grass, or dirt. First, remember that infants use their sensitive mouths as a tool to explore and learn. Your goal is to supervise well enough such that you can prevent your baby from mouthing potentially hazardous objects by gently using your hand to stop them before it happens: "You want to put the stick in your mouth, but I can't let you. That's not safe." Then you can gently remove the stick and provide an acceptable substitute, such as a teether.

However, the reality is that you aren't always going to be able to catch your baby before it happens. Sometimes, they're going to end up with a bit of grass or dirt in their mouth.

Instead of scolding your infant or suddenly exclaiming, "Ew! Get that out of your mouth," which unnecessarily communicates an emergency, try to take a breath and remain calm while offering gentle guidance: "You put that stick in your mouth, but I can't let you do that. It's not safe." Then gently remove the stick from your baby's hands. If necessary, you can also clean any remaining dirt from your baby's mouth, but be sure to kindly and respectfully let them know what you're doing: "I'm going to wipe this dirt out of your mouth now."

Also, know that this situation may happen many, many times (likely into toddlerhood) before your child eventually gets the message. But as always, do your best to exercise patience, and take it in stride each time.

TODDLERS

THE CHILD'S WALK

When adults go out for a walk, it is usually with some sort of goal in mind—to be back within the hour for lunch, to get to the park for a playdate, or perhaps to finish our obligatory 30 minutes of exercise for the day. However, our young children have not yet acquired an appreciation for such goals.

The wonderful thing about toddlers is that they live in the present, moving from one singular moment in time to the next, just as a butterfly flits from flower to flower. A young child's focus typically remains on the process involved in any task, without much consideration for the final outcome. If you've ever taken a walk outside with a toddler, then you know this to be an obvious truth: they will stop to investigate everything that catches their eye, from the lowly ant meandering across the sidewalk to the sudden sound of an airplane overhead.

We must realize that toddlers are naturally wired for this kind of deep curiosity and investigation; at this age, it is essentially their sole driving force. Instead of rushing our toddlers through each day in order to maintain a schedule, we must make a concerted effort to *slow down*, even adjusting our schedule to create more time to do so.

A simple way to make slowing down a regular part of your routine is to set aside an hour each day to take a *child's walk* outside in nature with your toddler. This is a walk determined only by the pace of your child, during which they are free to stop and investigate anything that catches their attention for as long as they'd like (within reason, of course, because you do have to get back home eventually). The primary goal is to avoid constantly rushing your toddler to "keep going" and instead to simply follow their lead. The specific location of your walk doesn't have to be an elaborate hike through the woods,

either. (Although this is certainly a great option if you happen to live near an open space.) It could be as simple as a walk through your neighbourhood or a visit to your local park. And even if you are limited on available green space, a walk down the street will still be able to provide fresh air and sunshine, a few trees, birds flying overhead, and perhaps the discovery of a flower growing out of a crack in the pavement. If you look and listen closely enough (because your toddler certainly is), then you'll quickly realize that nature can be found everywhere.

During a child's walk, you may notice that your toddler wants to climb or take other physical risks that cause you to feel a bit out of your comfort zone. And while your child's safety is always your first priority, try to allow your child to indulge these natural urges whenever possible. Obviously, if there is any potential for serious injury, then you can remain close to your child to "spot" while they explore, but otherwise, try to take as much of a hands-off approach as possible.

Just because it's raining, it doesn't mean you can't go outside. As the popular Scandinavian saying goes: *"There's no such thing as bad weather, only bad clothing."* So grab your raincoat, slip into a pair of rainboots, and let your child have a blast splashing in the puddles on your walk! As long as there are no imminent dangers in the weather conditions (e.g., lightning or dangerously low/high temperatures), then your child will benefit just as much from their daily walk as they would on any ordinary sunny afternoon.

PRESCHOOLERS

ENVIRONMENTAL STEWARDSHIP

During a child's first three years, much time is spent exploring the environment and gaining knowledge through the senses. Everything is learned quite passively and effortlessly, without the child's conscious awareness of the learning that is occurring. But as a child enters the preschool years, they become more consciously aware of the world around them. Almost as if a switch has been flipped, they are suddenly quite cognizant of their existence as an individual separate from others. They begin to ask questions and actively seek out specific experiences that will help them to understand more about the world. This is part of a classic intellectual transition, observed by Dr. Montessori, when a child passes into a new stage of development—from the *unconscious* absorbent mind (zero to three years) to the *conscious* absorbent mind (three to six years). Your child's positive experiences with the natural world during these early years will have a really strong impact on their attitude toward the environment as they grow older. And it makes sense that this should be the case. If a child is given plenty of opportunity to spend quality time outdoors exploring and interacting with nature, they are much more likely to find value in its preservation. Thus, it is crucial that you continue to foster experiences for your child that will contribute to this overarching goal throughout their childhood.

One of the easiest ways to encourage your preschool child's sense of environmental stewardship is to ensure that they spend plenty of free time outside each day, beyond any structured activities, like organized sports.

Your preschooler is ready and eager to learn about the world beyond your home, too! Offer a variety of activities, such as:

- hiking on a local trail
- spending time at the beach, lake, or mountains
- taking a tour of a local farm
- shopping for produce at your local farmers market
- participating in a community cleanup event
- participating in a local habitat restoration project
- taking a field trip to a recycling plant
- participating in a community garden
- visiting a plant nursery to start a backyard garden (or a patio container garden)
- starting a compost bin at home
- maintaining a bird feeder
- bird watching
- visiting a local botanical garden
- traveling to see a natural wonder
- camping in a local or national park

Your modeling and influence will have one of the greatest impacts on your child's eventual worldviews, so it is important that you participate in these activities alongside your child. They need to see that you find value and importance in the preservation of the environment. And as your child moves into future stages of development, they will have many wonderfully motivating experiences to draw upon when they begin taking a more independently active role in caring for the planet.

COMMON QUESTIONS

HOW CAN I HELP MY CHILD LEARN TO CLEAN UP THEIR TOYS?

Learning to clean up is a very gradual process. Beginning from infancy, it is essential to model putting away an activity after your child is done using it so that they can observe this as the normal way of doing things. Once your child reaches toddlerhood, it should become a collaborative process whereby you can invite their participation: "I'm going to put away the blocks. What would you like to put away?" And as a preschooler, even though your child will be much more capable of cleaning up independently, they will still require gentle reminders from you. (And yes, you'll still need to assist at times.)

IS THERE A MONTESSORI APPROACH TO SCREEN TIME?

Yes and no. Screens didn't exist in Dr. Montessori's time; therefore, she offered no advice about this. However, we can use what we've learned from Dr. Montessori about child development to guide us in adapting an approach that works for our individual families. We know that children learn best from hands-on experiences and live interaction with other people. Screens simply cannot replicate these experiences in quite the same way. Thus, for infants, toddlers, and preschoolers, it is best to have either no screen time at all (especially under the age of two) or a very limited amount of screen time that is monitored by a parent (for example, less than one hour per day).

HOW CAN I ENCOURAGE MY CHILD TO PLAY INDEPENDENTLY?

Your child *does not* need you to play the role of constant entertainer each day. What they *actually* need is for you to set up the environment, then step back and trust that they will find something to do on their own. Boredom is a gift, as it provides the opportunity for your child to follow their own interests and discover their creativity. And if your child is already accustomed to being entertained, then hit the reset button by starting small: leave the room for a quick bathroom break or to grab a cup of coffee before returning again. Gradually, you can increase the length of these trips while your child is playing until they are able to play independently for longer stretches of time.

HOW SHOULD I RESPOND WHEN MY CHILD BECOMES FRUSTRATED?

At times, your child may express frustration when trying to complete a difficult task (e.g., while playing with a new toy or getting dressed). Resist the urge to rescue or fix the problem for your child, as this will only communicate that you believe they are incapable of doing it themselves. If you feel a need to say something, then simply validate their feelings: "That puzzle is really hard for you." Don't intervene unless your child asks for help, and if they do, only show them a small step: "Sure, what part do you need help with? Hmm . . . I wonder if you turned the piece this way . . . " If your child gives up entirely, you can say: "That was really frustrating for you. It's okay to take a break and try again later."

WHAT IF MY CHILD ISN'T INTERESTED IN THEIR SHELF ACTIVITIES?

One of the core tenets of the Montessori approach is to observe and follow your child's lead. If you've noticed your child isn't spending much time engaged with the activities that are on the shelf, then you may need to spend some time observing. Perhaps the activities are too easy, too challenging, or have been out for too long and your child is bored with their choices. In these cases, a quick rotation for more appropriate activities can easily rejuvenate their interest in shelf work. However, children also go through periods during which they are more engaged by gross-motor activity. If you suspect this may be the culprit, then try to remain patient, and know that your child's interests in shelf activities will eventually return.

HOW CAN I HELP MY CHILD LEARN TO INTERACT SAFELY WITH PETS?

Pets can be unpredictable at times, so supervision is key in keeping your child safe. Stay nearby, and if you notice your child becoming too rough with a pet, be ready to kindly and firmly redirect the behavior by physically stopping their hand, then say something like, "I won't let you pull the dog's ear. That hurts the dog. Pet gently like this," and model for your child how to do so. If you need to temporarily leave your child unattended with a pet nearby, be sure to place your child in a separate, safe space until you are able to supervise again. (For example, you might use a baby gate or close a door to prevent the pet from entering.)

IS IT POSSIBLE TO CONTINUE OUR MONTESSORI ROUTINES WHILE TRAVELING?

While you may not be able to recreate every part of your normal home environment, you can certainly still maintain many of your normal routines. Depending on the length of your trip, you might bring along several familiar items that are part of your child's routines, such as their own placemat, silverware, and cup for mealtimes or their favorite books for bedtime. You can also continue providing opportunities for your child's independence. For example, they might enjoy wearing their own small backpack of essentials through the airport and choosing their own outfit each morning of the trip. Just focus on doing what you can to keep things familiar and offering freedom within limits wherever possible.

CAN I SET UP A MONTESSORI HOME WITH MULTIPLE CHILDREN?

In authentic Montessori classrooms, children are purposefully grouped into three-year age spans. The beauty of this arrangement is that younger children can learn from older children, while the older children reinforce their own learning each time they help the younger ones with a task they've already mastered. It is easy to see how the experience for siblings in a home environment is quite similar and actually best reflects a true Montessori environment. Just be sure to consider the safety of babies and toddlers who are not yet ready to handle materials intended for older siblings by keeping small parts out of reach of the younger ones, either on a higher shelf or in a container that is only accessible to the older sibling or in a separate area entirely.

IS THE MONTESSORI APPROACH EFFECTIVE FOR CHILDREN WITH SPECIAL NEEDS?

Yes! Children with special needs often require a caring, patient adult who is readily able to observe and anticipate their needs. They also learn best when offered concrete, hands-on learning experiences that are appropriate for their unique level of development, as well as the opportunity to move at their own pace, independent of other children. Conveniently enough, this is exactly the kind of environment that is provided in the Montessori approach for every child. Try not to compare your child to others. Instead, focus on finding ways to help your child experience independence at their unique level of ability, as well as offering developmentally appropriate, hands-on activities that are aligned with their needs and interests.

HOW DO I GET MY PARTNER/FAMILY/NANNY ON BOARD WITH MONTESSORI?

If you're excited about the idea of practicing Montessori at home but the other adults in your child's life aren't quite there yet, the most effective approach is going to be twofold: modeling and education. Share some of your favorite books, articles, and videos to help them learn more about the Montessori approach. You'll have a greater opportunity to influence their attitude and open-mindedness if they first have a clearer understanding of what it's all about. You can also have a greater impact by modeling it for them at every opportunity: speaking authentically and respectfully to your child at their eye level, offering limited choices, inviting your child's participation in practical life work, and creating spaces that foster independence. Remember that our actions speak much louder than our words.

HOW DO I MANAGE RECEIVING NON-MONTESSORI GIFTS FOR MY CHILD FROM OTHERS?

Your best course of action is actually to preempt the possibility of receiving these kinds of gifts by gently offering suggestions. You might mention your desire to pare down your child's toys at home, and ask instead for the gift of family experiences (e.g., zoo tickets) or a contribution to one larger group gift (e.g., a new bike). You can also create a gifting theme by asking all gifters to choose a favorite book to add to your child's library, or let them know which toys really engage your child right now (e.g., books and puzzles). You can also create an online wishlist that gifters can choose from, being sure to include only those items that you'd find acceptable, or consider requesting the gift of a Montessori-friendly subscription service. And if you still receive something you're not thrilled about, it's okay. Just graciously accept the gift, and worry about what to do with it at a later time.

CAN I STILL DO MONTESSORI AT HOME IF MY CHILD DOESN'T GO TO A MONTESSORI SCHOOL?

Of course! Even if a child attends a traditional school, the greatest influence on their attitudes and perspectives will always circle back to their parent(s) and lifestyle at home. At its heart, Montessori is about offering children the respect they deserve by creating opportunities for independence, offering freedom within limits, and nurturing their curiosity and desire to learn. These are things that can be done *anywhere* and most certainly *should be* a part of any home environment that is steeped in unconditional love and respect.

MONTESSORI FURNITURE & MATERIALS

When designing the various spaces around your home to align with Montessori principles, don't forget to begin by assessing what you may already have on hand. It's quite possible that some of your existing furniture, toys, and other materials could be easily repurposed or modified to create perfectly functional tools and spaces that support your child's independence and learning.

You can also find really great bargains on gently used items when you shop secondhand in thrift stores, consignment shops, yard sales, and many of the online marketplaces found on social media and various mobile apps. You might also consider doing some research to find a local toy swap group with other families in your area, where you can get new-to-you toys while also clearing out any items your child has outgrown.

Online Shops

Sprout (sprout-kids.com)
Beautiful, sustainably produced wooden furniture for every area of your home, thoughtfully designed with your child's needs in mind.

Manine Montessori (manine-montessori.com)
Furniture and materials to help you create a beautiful environment, adapted to the development and the interests of your child.

For Small Hands (forsmallhands.com)
A wide selection of hard-to-find, child-sized items that support your child's self-confidence and independence, from practical life materials to open-ended games, toys, and crafts.

Montessori Services (montessoriservices.com)
Specialized furniture and materials for Montessori homes and classrooms, including intriguing toys, tools, games, crafts, and books to help you create a rich, authentic environment.

Alison's Montessori (alisonsmontessori.com)
Comprehensive learning materials that will nurture your child's ability to absorb information and work to their full potential, available at a range of price points to suit your unique budget.

Nienhuis Montessori (nienhuis.com)
Authentic Montessori learning materials and furniture for children ages 0 to 12 years, founded in 1929 in collaboration with Dr. Montessori and officially endorsed by the Association Montessori Internationale (AMI).

Montessori & Me (montessoriandme.us)
Wooden, heirloom-quality, Montessori-inspired materials and furniture for babies, toddlers, and preschoolers.

Toki Mats (tokimats.com)
Super soft, washable play mats for your little one's play space, made of 100 percent natural materials and available in a variety of modern designs.

Etsy (etsy.com)
Support small businesses in your search to find beautiful, high-quality, handmade furniture and materials to add to your home.

- BellasCasa
- EssentialMontessori
- FromJennifer
- HeirLoomKidsUSA
- MakaArtCrafts
- MakShopForKids
- MamaPsPlaceLLC
- MimiaMontessori
- MontessoriVita
- WoodAndHearts

Ikea (ikea.com)
Lots of unique, Montessori-friendly children's furniture, shelving, and materials at great prices.

Amazon (amazon.com)
An ever-expanding selection of furniture and materials for every area of your home, offered at a variety of price points and shipped directly to your door.

DIY Options

If you fancy the idea of spending a few hours (or weekends!) working on a DIY project, you can find an endless array of tutorials online. Here are some ideas to get started:

Activity shelf: tinyurl.com/5caa9mev

Floor bed: tinyurl.com/2jrmwemb

Weaning table: tinyurl.com/ea4rwu9k

Learning tower: tinyurl.com/483zn63e

Front-facing bookshelf: tinyurl.com/ku2bdwwr

Montessori baby mobiles

- Munari: tinyurl.com/7vrdtuae
- Octahedron: tinyurl.com/6epwyj5j
- Gobbi: tinyurl.com/aszwvf9a
- Dancers: tinyurl.com/thmhf7zj

Visual recipes for cooking: tinyurl.com/ue8ef5pm

Subscription Services

Some families may also enjoy the convenience of signing up for a subscription-based toy service, such as **Monti Kids** (an authentic Montessori program for 0–3 years old) or **Lovevery** (Montessori-inspired play kits for 0–4 years old). These services can help to take the guesswork out of parenting, as they curate developmentally appropriate activities that are delivered right to your home.

RECOMMENDED READING & RESOURCES

Books

The Absorbent Mind by Maria Montessori

The Secret of Childhood by Maria Montessori

Dr. Montessori's Own Handbook by Maria Montessori

The Joyful Child: Montessori, Global Wisdom for Birth to Three by Susan Mayclin Stephenson

Montessori from the Start: The Child at Home, from Birth to Age Three by Paula Polk Lillard and Lynn Lillard Jessen

How to Raise an Amazing Child the Montessori Way by Tim Seldin

The Montessori Toddler by Simone Davies

The Montessori Baby by Simone Davies and Junnifa Uzodike

Teach Me to Do It Myself by Maja Pitamic

No Bad Kids: Toddler Discipline Without Shame by Janet Lansbury

Positive Discipline: The First Three Years by Jane Nelsen

Positive Discipline for Preschoolers by Jane Nelsen

No-Drama Discipline by Daniel J. Siegel and Tina Payne Bryson

Siblings Without Rivalry by Adele Faber

How to Talk So Little Kids Will Listen by Joanna Faber

Unconditional Parenting by Alfie Kohn

Simplicity Parenting by Kim John Payne

Cooking Class: 57 Fun Recipes That Kids Will Love to Make by Deanna F. Cook

Cooking Class Global Feast!: 44 Recipes that Celebrate the World's Cultures by Deanna F. Cook

Online Resources from the Author

"Montessori at Home" YouTube video series: tinyurl.com/4awdd9nr

"Montessori at Home" and "Positive Discipline Parenting" self-paced e-courses: montessori-at-home.teachable.com

Montessori Printables: teacherspayteachers.com/Store/Hapa-Family-Montessori

Montessori and parenting blog articles: ashley-yeh.com

INDEX

A

Absorbent Mind, The, 14

absorbent mind, period of, 22

activities
  infant activities, 100–106
  preschool activities, 116–123
  presenting of, 94–95
  toddler activities, 107–115

adolescence (plane of development), 23

adult. *See* prepared adult

arts and crafts materials, 84–85

Avocado Toast & Egg, 58

B

Banana Bread, 63

bathroom, 38–47
  infants, 40–41
  preschoolers, 46–47
    achieving independence, 46–47
    privacy, 47
  toddlers, 42–45
    access to water and toiletries, 42
    bathing, 44
    cleaning fingernails, 44
    handwashing, 42–44
    toilet learning, 44–45
    toothbrushing, 44

bedroom, 26–37
  decor, 27
  independence, 27
  infants, 28–31
    artwork (low wall), 31

book basket, 31
caregiver's chair, 31
changing area, 31
clothing storage, 31
floor bed, 28–30
infant shelf, 31
optional elements, 31
preschoolers, 36–37
  access to clothing, 36
  artwork (low wall), 37
  care-of-self area, 36
  floor or raised bed, 36
  light switch, 37
  preschooler shelf, 36–37
  reading area, 37
toddlers, 32–35
  access to clothing, 34–35
  artwork (low wall), 35
  care-of-self area, 34
  floor bed, 32–33
  light switch, 35
  reading area, 35
  toddler shelf, 35

Berry Sunrise Smoothie, 58

Black Bean Quesadillas, 59

brushing teeth. *See* toothbrushing

Burrito Bowl, 63

C

care of environment
  preschoolers, 138–139
    flower arranging, 138
    polishing wood, 139
    tending a garden, 138
    using real tools, 139
  toddlers, 131–133
    dusting, sweeping, and mopping, 133
    folding napkins or

cloths, 133
pet care, 133
plant care, 133
table setting and clearing, 133
table washing, 133
washing dishes, 133
window washing, 133

care of self
  preschoolers, 136–137
    braiding, 136–137
    food preparation, 137
    making the bed, 136
    sewing, 136
    using clothespins, 136
    using office supplies, 137
  toddlers, 128–131
    dressing frames, 130
    food preparation, 131
    independent dressing, 128–130
    laundry, 130–131
    Montessori "Coat Flip," 130
    personal hygiene, 128

care-of-self area
  preschoolers, 36
  toddlers, 34

child, 22–25
  absorbent mind, 22
  four planes of development, 22–23
    adolescence, 23
    childhood, 23
    infancy, 22–23
    maturity, 23
  freedom, need for, 25
  maximum effort, 25
  sensitive periods, 24

childhood
  plane of development, 23
  secret of, 13

child's work. *See* play space

choice, freedom of, 25

common questions, 150–153

D

development, four planes of, 22–23
  adolescence, 23
  childhood, 23
  infancy, 22–23
  maturity, 23

dining area, 64–75
  grace and courtesy, 74–75
  infants, 66–69
    cutlery, 67
    drinking from open cup, 68
    exploring food, 68–69
    weaning table, 66–67
  preschoolers, 74–75
  social aspects, 65
  toddlers, 70–73
    junior chair, 70
    mealtime behavior expectations, 73
    refining skills, 71–72
    setting the table, 72

E

Easy Cheesy Muffins, 62

eating. *See* dining area

effort, maximum, 25

entryway, 48–51
  cooperation, 51
  as critical space, 49
  setup, 50–51

environment. *See* care of environment; prepared environment essential triad (foundation), 13–25

child, 22–25
  absorbent mind, 22
  four planes of development, 22–23
  freedom, need for, 25
  maximum effort, 25
  sensitive periods, 24

prepared adult, 14–16
  feedback and encouragement, 16
  freedom within limits, 15–16
  observation, 14–15
  respect, 15

prepared environment, 18–21
  decluttering and organizing, 19–20
  description of environment, 18
  independence, opportunities for, 20
  natural elements, 21
  reality, foundation of, 20–21

F–G–H

food preparation. See kitchen

foundation. See essential triad (foundation)

four planes of development, 22–23
  adolescence, 23
  childhood, 23
  infancy, 22–23
  maturity, 23

freedom, need for, 25

getting dressed. See care of self

grace and courtesy, 74–75

great outdoors, 142–149
  infants, 144–145
  preschoolers, 149
  toddlers, 146–147

I–J

infancy (plane of development), 22–23

infant activities, 100–106
  ball cylinder, 104
  cards in a wallet, 105
  circle shape knobbed puzzle, 103
  egg in cup and peg in cup, 104
  grasping beads, 100
  high-contrast cards, 101
  in-and-out work, 104
  infant coin box, 105
  interlocking discs, 102
  language basket, 105
  musical instruments, 102
  newborn rattle, 100
  object permanence box, 104
  pincer grasp block, 105
  pull toy, 106
  scarf box, 102
  sensory balls, 101
  sensory fabrics, 103
  sensory shakers, 103
  small bell cylinder, 101
  spinning drum, 101
  themed treasure basket, 103

walker wagon, 106
wooden ring stacker, 102

infants
  bathroom, 40–41
  bedroom, 28–31
    artwork (low wall), 31
    book basket, 31
    caregiver's chair, 31
    changing area, 31
    clothing storage, 31
    floor bed, 28–30
    infant shelf, 31
    optional elements, 31
  dining area, 66–69
    cutlery, 67
    drinking from open cup, 68
    exploring food, 68–69
    weaning table, 66–67
  great outdoors, 144–145
  kitchen, 54
  practical life for, 126–127

infant shelf, 31, 79

Itard, Jean Marc Gaspard, 10

K

kitchen, 52–63
  curiosity about, 53
  infants, 54
  preschoolers, 60–63
    breakfast preparation, 60
    food preparation, 137
    recipes for, 62–63
    visual recipes, 60–61
  toddlers, 55–59
    access to kitchen tools and serveware, 55
    food preparation, 131
    independent snack

selection, 56
learning tower, 56
recipes for, 58–59

L

learning tower, 56

life skills (practical), 124–141
  infants, 126–127
  preschoolers, 136–141
    care of environment, 138–139
    care of self, 136–137
    grace and courtesy, 140–141
  toddlers, 128–135
    care of environment, 131–133
    care of self, 128–131
    general housework, 131–133
    transfer work, 134–135

M–N–O

maturity (plane of development), 23

maximum effort, 25

mealtime. See dining area

Montessori "Coat Flip," 130

Montessori, Dr. Maria, 9, 10–11

Montessori furniture and materials (sources), 154–155

Montessori lifestyle, advantages of, 8

Montessori Method, 11

Montessori puzzle ball, 99

Montessori tactile mobiles, 99

Montessori visual mobiles, 98

dancers mobile (8–12 weeks old), 98

Gobbi mobile (7–10 weeks old), 98

Munari mobile (3–6 weeks old), 98

octahedron mobile (5–8 weeks old), 98

movement, freedom of, 25

nature, connecting with. *See* great outdoors

Oatmeal Chocolate Chip Cookies, 59

P–Q

play space, 76–123

activity, presenting of, 94–95

example, 94–95

show (don't tell), 94

books

choosing, 86–87

rotation, 89

design of, 78–81

aesthetic considerations, 80

furnishings (other), 79–80

infant shelf, 79

mantra (less is more), 78

shelving, 79

infant activities, 100–106

infant's movement area, 96–99

preschool activities, 116–123

shelf organization, 90–91

categories, 90–91

shelf map, 90

shelf rotation and toy storage, 88–89

child's interests, 88

expectations (toy storage), 88–89

toddler activities, 107–115

toys and activities, selection of, 82–85

arts and crafts materials, 84–85

battery-operated toys, avoidance of, 82

close-ended activities, 83

gross-motor movement, 84

natural materials, 82

open-ended materials, 83–84

opportunities to support, 84

work tray, arrangement of, 92–93

aesthetics, 93

left to right, 93

undone activities, 92

potty training. *See* toilet learning

practical life. *See* life skills (practical)

prepared adult, 14–16

feedback and encouragement, 16

freedom within limits, 15–16

observation, 14–15

respect, 15

prepared environment, 18–21

decluttering and organizing, 19–20

description of environment, 18

independence, opportunities for, 20

natural elements, 21

reality, foundation of, 20–21

preschool activities, 116–123

activity words game, 118

audio books, 119

board games, 123

"Bring me" game, 119

cards and counters, 120

categories, 117

classical music appreciation, 122

classifying vertebrate animals, 122

coin matching, 120

color grading, 116

color mixing, 123

daily calendar, 120

fabric matching, 117

geoboard, 116

living vs. non-living, 121

magnetic vs. non-magnetic, 121

opposites, 118

pin punching, 123

plants vs. animals, 122

rhyming words, 117

sand tray, 119

secret messages game, 118

sequencing life cycles, 121

sink or float, 122

sound blending game, 118

sound matching, 117

sprouting seeds, 121

three-part cards, 119

using a ruler, 120

yoga cards, 123

preschoolers

bathroom, 46–47

achieving independence, 46–47

privacy, 47

bedroom, 36–37

access to clothing, 36

artwork (low wall), 37

care-of-self area, 36

floor or raised bed, 36

light switch, 37

preschooler shelf, 36–37

reading area, 37

dining area, 74–75

great outdoors, 149

kitchen, 60–63

breakfast preparation, 60

recipes for, 62–63

visual recipes, 60–61

practical life for, 136–141

care of environment, 138–139

care of self, 136–137

grace and courtesy, 140–141

preschooler shelf, 36–37

R–S

recipes

for preschoolers, 62–63

Banana Bread, 63

Burrito Bowl, 63

Easy Cheesy Muffins, 62

Turkey Ranch Wrap, 62

for toddlers, 58–59

Avocado Toast & Egg, 58

Berry Sunrise Smoothie, 58

Black Bean Quesadillas, 59

Oatmeal Chocolate Chip Cookies, 59

repetition, freedom of, 25

Séguin, Édouard, 10

sensitive periods, 24

sleep. *See* bedroom

T–U–V

toddler activities, 107–115

ball pounding bench, 109

colored ring stacker, 107

color matching, 113

counting boards, 115

discs on a horizontal dowel, 109

fitting lids to containers, 107

gross-motor movement, 109

hammering, 114

imbucare box, 108

"I Spy" sound game, 115

jigsaw puzzles, 112

lacing beads, 111

lock and key, 112

locks and latches, 110

matching animal heads and tails, 114

matryoshka nesting dolls, 111

multiple shape knobbed puzzle, 108

mystery bag, 113

nesting boxes, cups, and bowls, 108

object-to-object matching, 110

object-to-picture matching, 112

1-to-1 correspondence, 111

open-and-close work, 108

picture-to-picture matching, 114

scissors/cutting, 113

shaker and toothpicks, 109

shape sorter, 110

small-knobbed peg puzzles, 110

sorting, 114

stacking boxes, 111

stacking peg board, 112

threading, 113

toddlers

bathroom, 42–45

access to water and toiletries, 42

bathing, 44

cleaning fingernails, 44

handwashing, 42–44

toothbrushing, 44

toilet learning, 44–45

bedroom, 32–35

access to clothing, 34–35

artwork (low wall), 35

care-of-self area, 34

floor bed, 32–33

light switch, 35

reading area, 35

toddler shelf, 35

dining area, 70–73

junior chair, 70

mealtime behavior expectations, 73

refining skills, 71–72

setting the table, 72

great outdoors, 146–147

kitchen, 55–59

access to kitchen tools and serveware, 55

independent snack selection, 56

learning tower, 56

recipes for, 58–59

practical life for, 128–135

care of environment, 131–133

care of self, 128–131

general housework, 131–133

transfer work, 134–135

toddler shelf, 35

toothbrushing, 44

toys and activities, selection of, 82–85

arts and crafts materials, 84–85

battery-operated toys, avoidance of, 82

close-ended activities, 83

gross motor movement,

natural materials, 82

open-ended materials, 83–84

opportunities to support, 84

Turkey Ranch Wrap, 62

W–X–Y–Z

waiting hand, 141

weaning table, 66–67

work space (child's). *See* play space

ACKNOWLEDGMENTS

My deepest gratitude goes first to my two beautiful girls, Kylie and Mia, who were the originating source of my passion for Montessori and without whom this book would never have come into being. You make my heart positively burst with love and pride each day, and I am so thankful to have a front-row seat to the amazing human beings that you are growing up to be.

I would also like to thank Mike, my endlessly wonderful husband and loving partner, for always encouraging me to follow my passions and working so hard to create the opportunities needed to make them happen.

I am also thankful for my mother, for having the love and determination to seek the best education for me as a child by enrolling me in a Montessori school. That decision was truly the one spark that started all of this, and I am eternally grateful.

Big thanks also goes to the wonderful team of editors and designers at DK, for believing in me and offering their support throughout the writing of this book. And also to my photographer, Hannah Quintana, for breathing life into the visual essence of Montessori.

And to all of my fellow Montessori parents, caregivers, educators, and advocates in the online world, I'd like to offer a BIG thank you—"from one busy parent to another"—for all of your inspiration and unwavering support and for sharing my work with your own loved ones across the globe.

ABOUT THE AUTHOR

Ashley Yeh, M.Ed., is a certified Montessori guide for infants and toddlers, is a Positive Discipline Parent Educator, and has spent several years working as an educator in public classrooms. She has a deep passion and respect for the Montessori approach, having raised her own two children from infancy using Montessori principles. Ashley has also inspired thousands of families around the world to bring Montessori into their homes via her YouTube channel, blog articles, and online courses.

YouTube: Hapa Family
Online Courses: montessori-at-home.teachable.com
Website: ashley-yeh.com
Instagram: @hapafamilyvlog